Nelson English

Copymaster Resource Book

BLUE LEVEL

John Jackman Wendy Wren

Published in 2001 by:
Nelson Thornes Ltd
Delta Place
27 Bath Road
CHELTENHAM
GL53 7TH
United Kingdom

01 02 03 04 05 / 10 9 8 7 6 5 4 3 2 1

A catalogue record for this book is available from the British Library

ISBN 0-17-424800-8

Illustrations by Geoff Ball, Denise Coble, Carol Daniel, Mike Lacey, Gilly Marklew, Stuart Martin, Terry Riley, Amelia Rosato, Lisa Smith, Andrew Tewson, Jenny Tulip, Mike Walsh, Amanda Wood
Page make-up by Clive Sutherland

Printed and bound in Croatia by Zrinski

The authors and publishers wish to thank the following for permission to use copyright material on the copymaster facsimiles:
Pie Corbett, 'Ice Lolly', first published in *Another Very First Poetry Book*, Oxford University Press, by permission of the author. John Foster, 'Sand', first published in *My Blue Poetry Book*, Macmillan (1988); copyright © John Foster 1988, by permission of the author. An extract from Malorie Blackman, 'Betsey's Birthday Surprise' from *Betsey Biggalow* by Malorie Blackman, Piccadilly Press; copyright © Malorie Blackman 1996, by permission of A M Heath & Co Ltd on behalf of the author. An extract from Nancy Blishen, 'A Little Bit of Colour' from *A Treasury of Stories for Five Year Olds* by Nancy Blishen; copyright © Nancy Blishen 1989, by permission of Kingfisher Publications Plc. Judith Nicholls, 'PE'; copyright © Judith Nicholls 1991, by permission of the author. 'I Had a Little Cherry Stone' from *Number Rhymes and Finger Plays* by Boyce and Bartlett, Pitman and Sons, by permission of Pearson Education. 'Who's in?', a poem by Elizabeth Fleming. 'One Hot Day', a poem by Tessa May.

Every effort has been made to trace copyright holders and to obtain their permission for the use of copyright material. The publishers will gladly receive any information enabling them to rectify any error or omission in subsequent editions.

Contents

Introduction

In this **Copymaster Resource Book**, two copymasters are supplied for use with each unit, as follows:

- Word skills copymaster
- Writing copymaster.

The copymasters are closely linked to the posters and may be used for support, consolidation, differentiation and extension.

Use the unit 'flag' on the side of each copymaster to help you turn quickly to the copymasters that are relevant to your current work. Fiction copymasters are marked with a black flag (unit number in white), non-fiction with a grey flag (unit number in black).

Four further copiable resources are included in this book – **Poster copymasters, Letter skills copymasters, Spelling Lists** and a **Pupil Record Sheet**.

The **Poster copymasters** are black-line facsimiles of the posters. Much of the work suggested in connection with the posters can be practised or extended using these copymasters. For example, children might be asked to circle target initial letters, underline significant words, etc. In addition, the copymasters may be taken home, allowing children to undertake further work with parents or guardians.

The **Letter skills copymasters** are provided to teach and/or revise and secure letter skills. These copymasters offer practice, sequentially, in:

- the more frequently used initial consonant letters
- the vowel letters
- letters that are frequently confused by younger children.

The **Spelling Lists** provided for each Fiction unit together comprise the key words children need to learn to spell at this age (National Literacy Strategy Appendix List 1), and are designed to be cut out and taken home by pupils so that they can practise the words at home.

The **Pupil Record Sheet** is designed for the recording of individual pupils' progress throughout each year as they work through the copymasters for each unit. You may choose to use this as the front cover of a storage folder for each child's work. This will enable you to keep together selected samples of work and will conveniently provide the necessary profiling evidence to document each child's progress.

Nelson English

Spelling Lists – Reception Year

Unit 1	Unit 2	Unit 3	Unit 4
I look a	to is he	and she it	we the can mum

Unit 5	Unit 6	Unit 7	Unit 8
dad in am see	on you at was	my up like for	said play cat dog

Unit 9	Unit 10	Unit 11	Unit 12
went go are me	big this day no	going come of away	they yes get all

Nelson English

Word Skills Copymaster 1

Blue: Fiction

name ______________________ date ______________________

Trace over the letters.

Colour the animals.

l l l

s s s

m m m

p p p

name ______________________ date ______________________

Trace over the dotted letters.

This is a big lion.

This is a bold lion.

This is a slippery snake.

This is a hissing snake.

This is a baby monkey.

This is a tiny monkey.

unit 1

Nelson English

Word Skills Copymaster 1

Blue: Non-fiction

name ______________________ date ______________________

Trace over the letters.

Colour the animals.

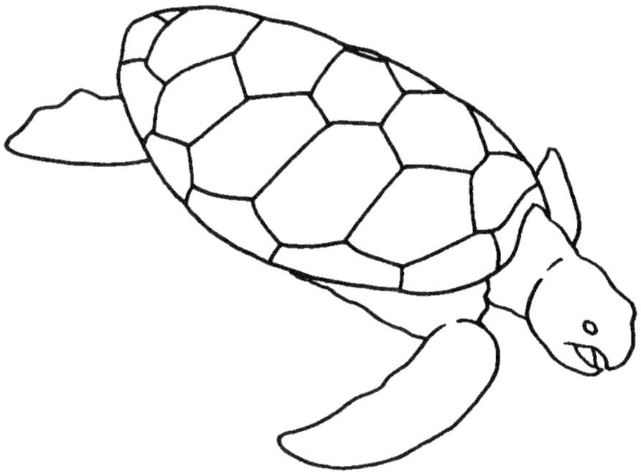

h h h

t t t

b b b

c c c

name ______________________ date ______________________

Trace over the letters.

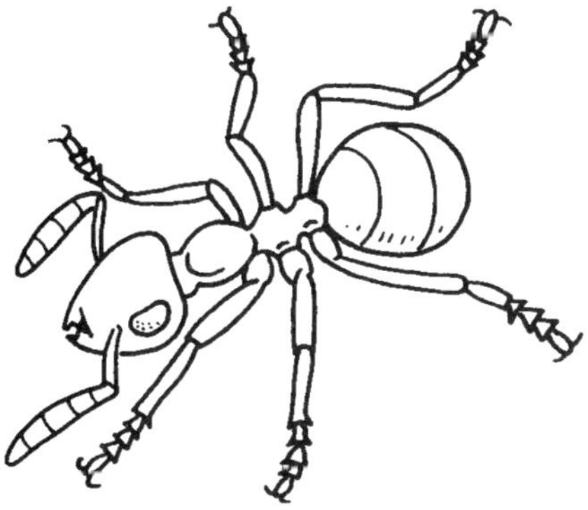

ant

frog

lion

rabbit

seal

zebra

Nelson English

Word Skills Copymaster 2

Blue: Fiction

name ____________________ date ____________________

unit 2

■ Say the name of each picture.
Circle the letter it begins with.

w f h

n m h

t q l

r g n

t s l

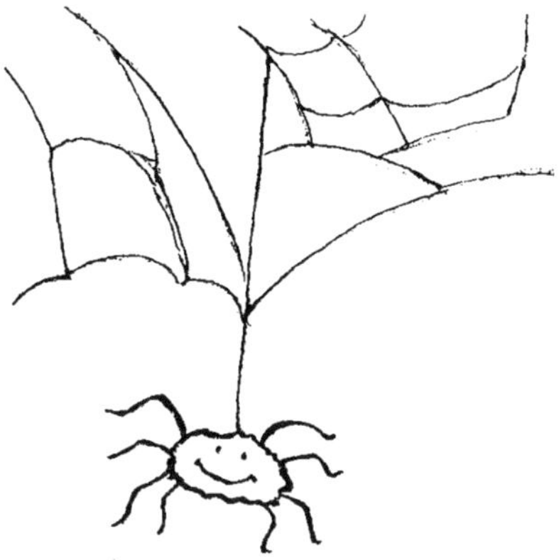

c s f

■ Write the first letter of each picture.

______ ______ ______ ______

Writing Copymaster 2

name ______________________ date ______________________

Write the names of the animals.
The words are in the box.

fly	dog	mice	kitten

d ___ ___

m ___ ___ ___

k ___ ___ ___ ___ ___

f ___ ___

name ____________________ date ____________________

unit 2

■ Sound the letters.
Copy the letter patterns.

at ________ ________ in ________ ________

ot ________ ________ ug ________ ________

■ Finish the words.
Colour the pictures.

c___ ___

h___ ___

t___ ___

b___ ___

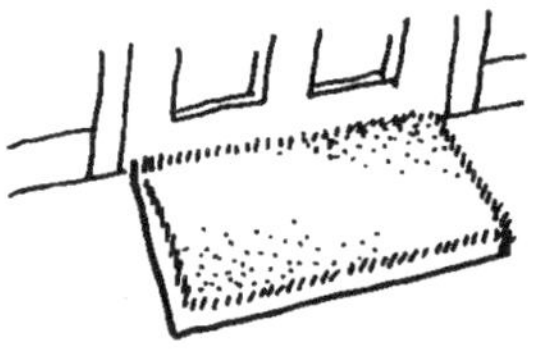
m___ ___

r___ ___

p___ ___

f___ ___

■ Make these words.

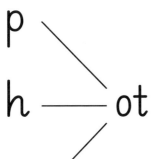

p		pot	m		mug
h	ot	________	j	ug	________
n		________	h		________

name ______________________ date ______________________

Label the pictures.

The words are in the box.

shelf	cup	sink
peg	door	table

p__ __

sh__ __ __

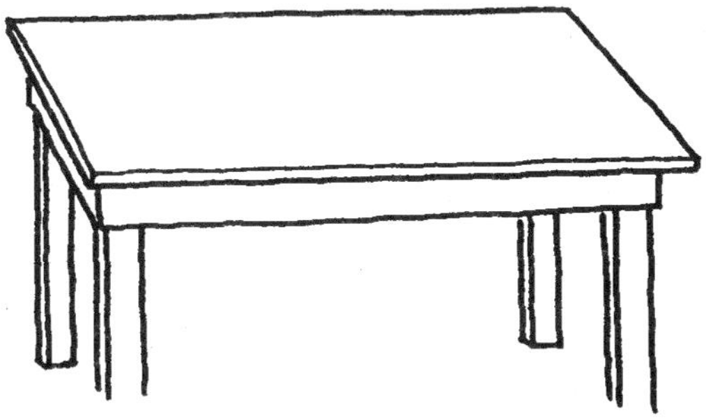

t__ __ __ __

s__ __ __

c__ __

d__ __ __

name ______________ date ______________

unit 3

Copy the words that rhyme.

bun	fit	fun	bed	sit	fed

red	sun	hit
______	______	______
______	______	______

For each word, write a rhyming word.
The pictures will help you.

mug

box

hen

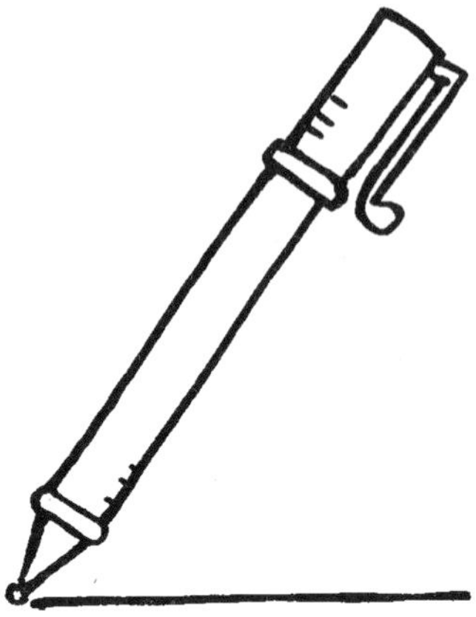

______ ______ ______

Writing Copymaster 3

name ______________________ date ______________________

■ Colour the greenhouse.

Show how Daniel and Tom painted it.

■ Write about your picture.

____

____

____

Word Skills Copymaster 3

name ______________________ date ______________________

Colour each word the correct colour.

Find the picture that goes with it.

Colour that picture the same colour as the word.

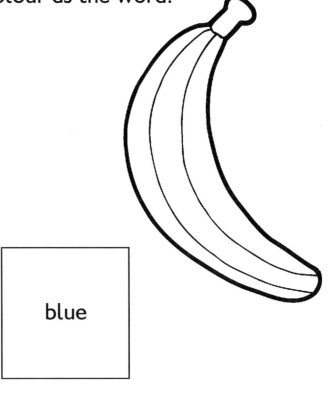

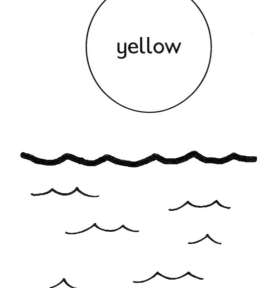

red

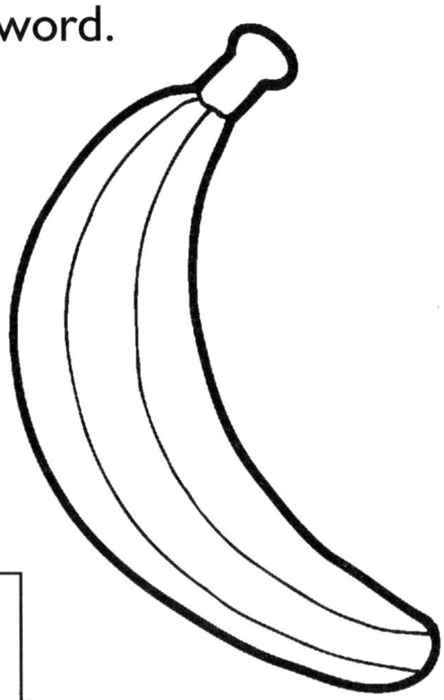

blue

yellow

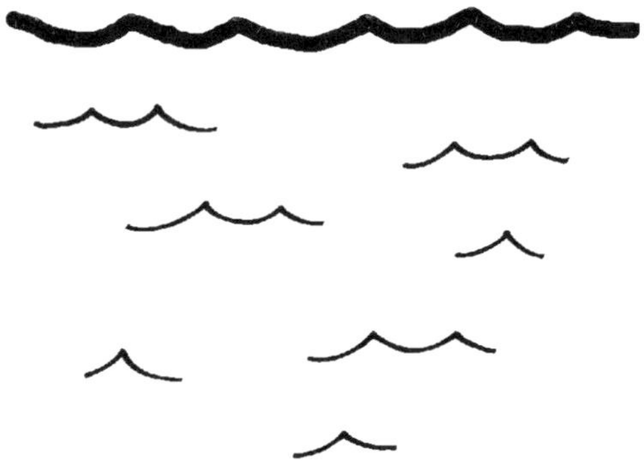

green

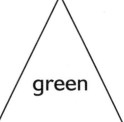

Writing Copymaster 3

name ______________________ date ______________________

■ Colour the picture.

Colour the **R** shapes **red**.
Colour the **Y** shapes **yellow**.
Colour the **G** shapes **green**.
Colour the **B** shapes **blue**.

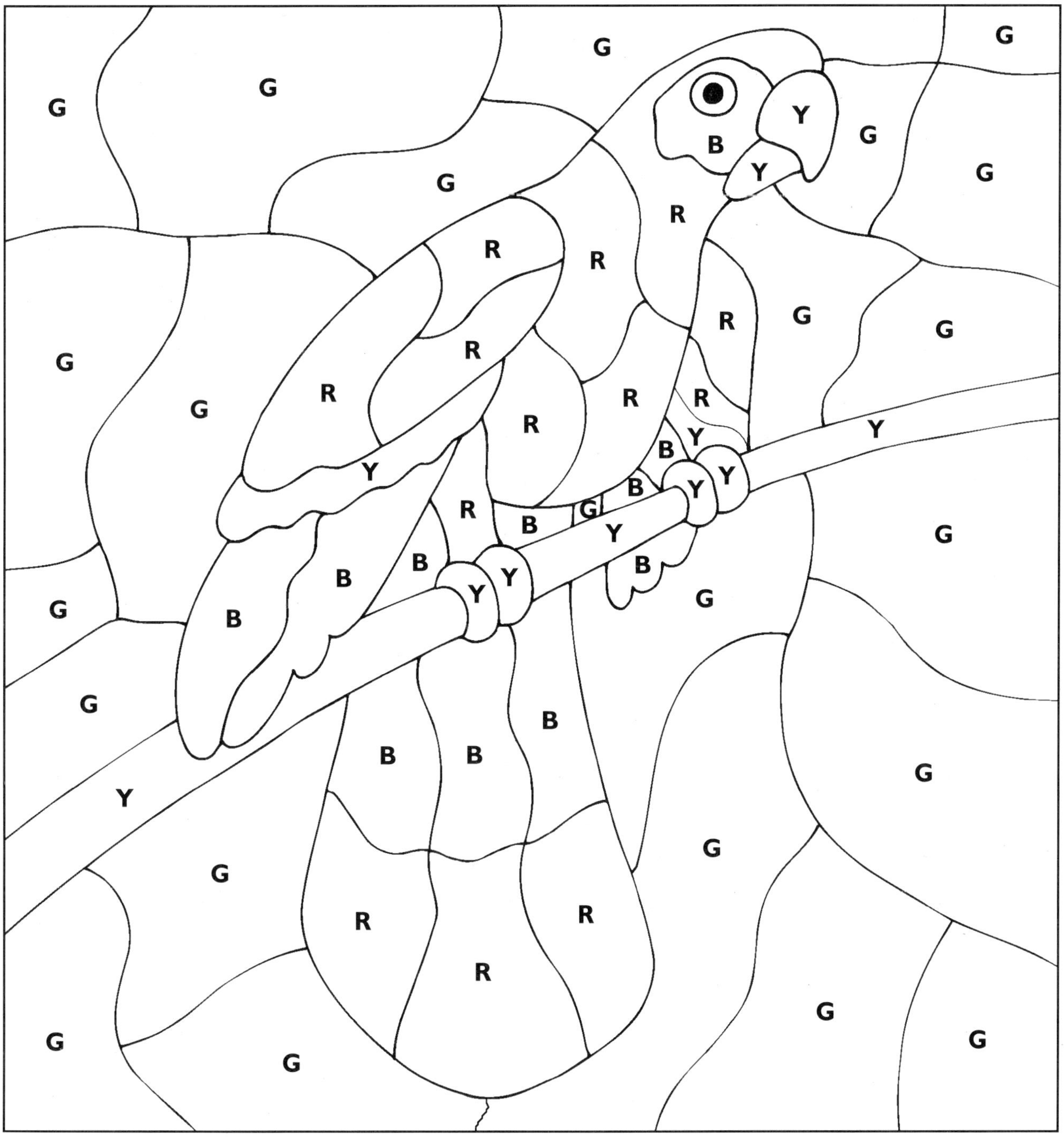

■ What is the picture?

____

Word Skills Copymaster 4

name ______________________ date ______________________

Start at 'a' and join the dots.

Fill in the missing letters.

a b ___ d ___ f g ___ i

j ___ l ___ n ___ p ___ r

s ___ u ___ w x ___ z

name ______________________ date ______________________

■ Put the pictures in the correct order.

There is a tiny shoot in the ground.

The shoot has grown into a tree.

The girl is planting a cherry stone.

The shoot has grown bigger.

■ Finish the sentence.

The pictures show ______________________

____

____.

Word Skills Copymaster 4

name ______________________ date ______________________

Colour each word a different colour.

Colour each picture to match the word it goes with.

spring

autumn

winter

summer

Writing Copymaster 4

name ______________________ date ______________________

Write about each picture.

____

____

____

____

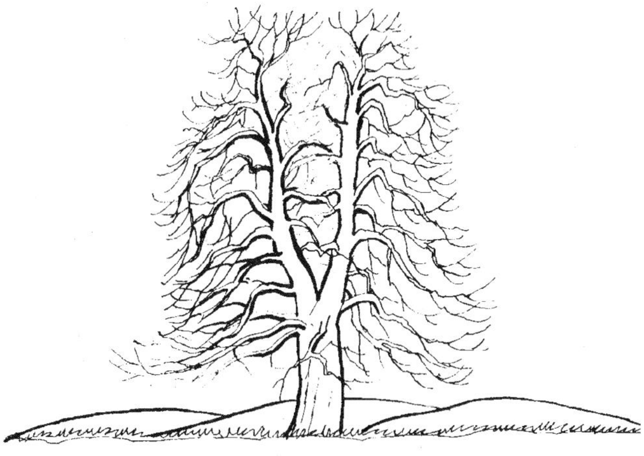

____

____

____

____

name ______________________ date ______________________

unit 5

■ Colour the four words that start with 'sh'.

s	m	o	s	r	t
h	p	s	h	i	p
e	s	h	e	d	l
e	j	s	l	o	e
p	q	j	l	t	h

■ Write each word you found under the correct picture.

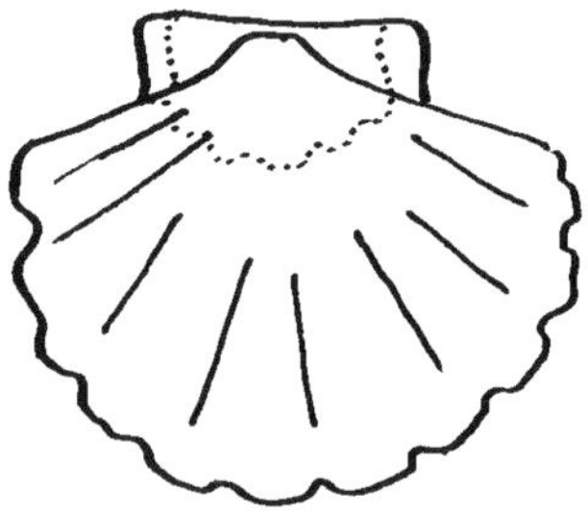

______________________ ______________________

______________________ ______________________

Writing Copymaster 5

Blue: Fiction

name ______________________ date ______________________

Think of something you like to do.
What do you want when you are doing it?

When I ______________________

I wear ______________________.

Draw a picture of the clothes.

Write about the clothes you have drawn.

____

____

____

unit 5

Nelson English

Word Skills Copymaster 5

Blue: Non-fiction

name ______________________ date ______________________

Join the words to the correct parts of the body.
The first one has been done to help you.

unit 5

name ______________________ date ______________________

My name is ______________________.

I am __________ years old.

My hair is ______________________.

My eyes are ______________________.

I am ______________ tall.

My favourite colour is ______________.

My favourite food is ______________.

Write about what you like doing.

____

____

____

Word Skills Copymaster 6

name ______________________ date ______________________

unit 6

A Start at 'A' and join the dots.

B Fill in the missing letters.

A ___ C ___ E F ___ H I

___ K ___ M N O ___ Q R

___ T U ___ W ___ Y Z

Nelson English

Writing Copymaster 6

Blue: Fiction

name ______________________ date ______________________

■ Colour the picture.

■ Write what is happening in the picture.

____

____

____

____

unit 6

Word Skills Copymaster 6

name ______________________ date ______________________

Colour each word a different colour.

Colour each picture to match the word it goes with.

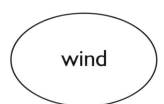

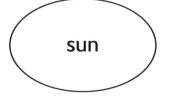

snow

wind

clouds

sun

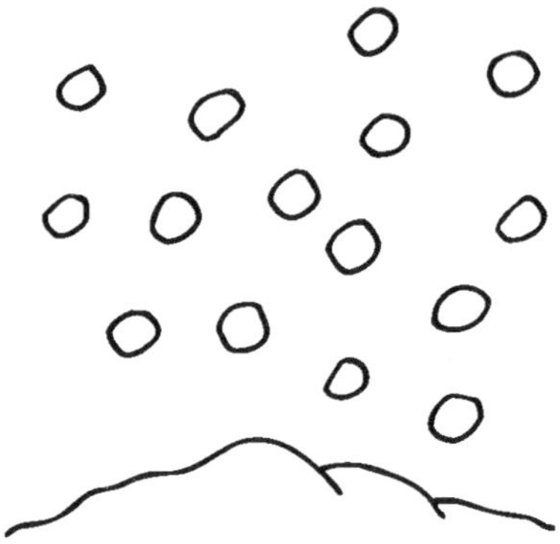

rain

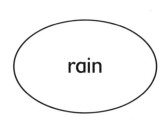

name ______________________ date ______________________

TODAY'S WEATHER

Day ______________________

Date ______________________

Month ______________________

Weather word ______________________

Weather picture

Weather sentence

____

____

Word Skills Copymaster 7

name ______________________ date ______________________

Draw lines to join the pairs of rhyming words.

The first one has been done to help you.

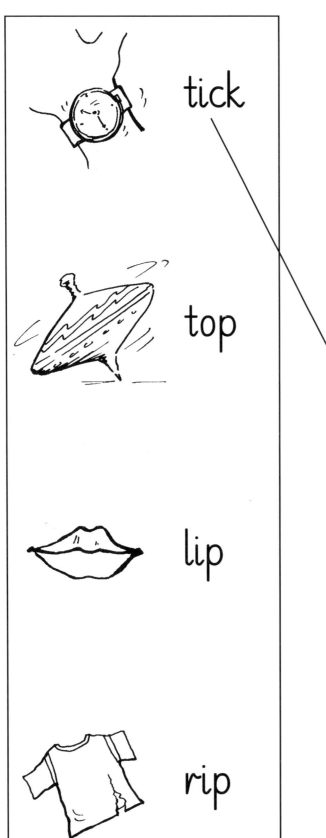

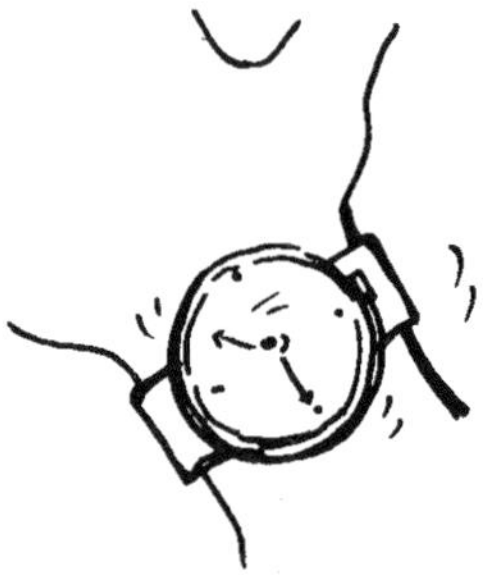

tick

top

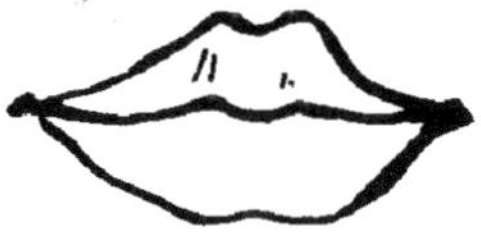

lip

rip

slip

drip

stick

stop

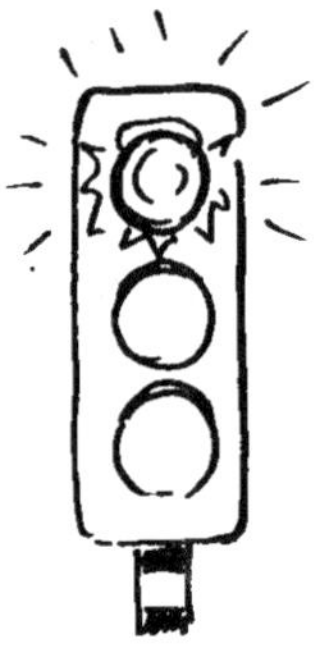

Writing Copymaster 7

name ______________________ date ______________________

Draw your ice lolly here.

What shape is your ice lolly?

____

What colour is your ice lolly?

____

What flavour is your ice lolly?

____

Word Skills Copymaster 7

name ______________________ date ______________________

■ Colour the four words that start with 'ch'.

m	c	h	i	p	s
c	h	e	e	s	e
l	c	h	a	i	r
c	h	e	r	r	y

■ Write each word you found under the right picture.

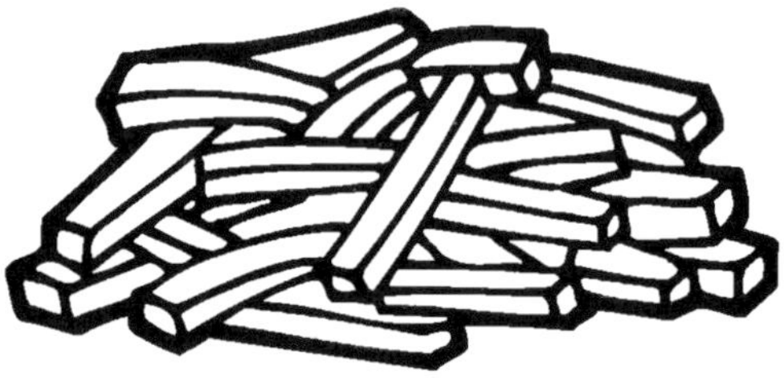

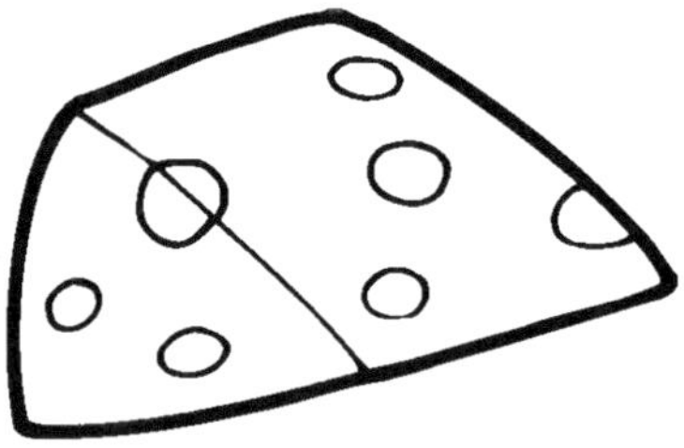

______________________ ______________________

______________________ ______________________

name ______________________ date ______________________

Finish the labels.

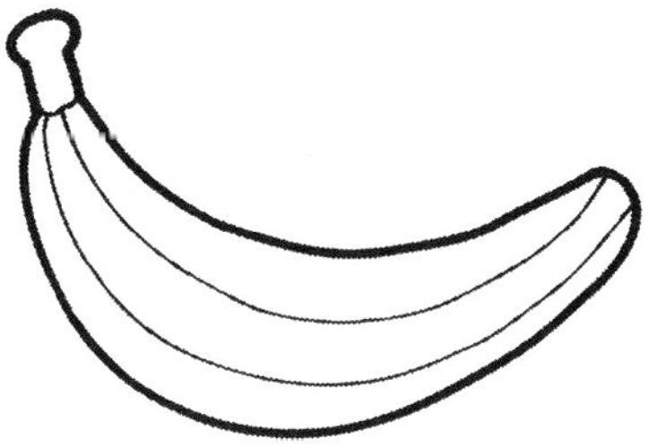

b _ _ _ _ _   p _ _ _ _   a _ _ _ _

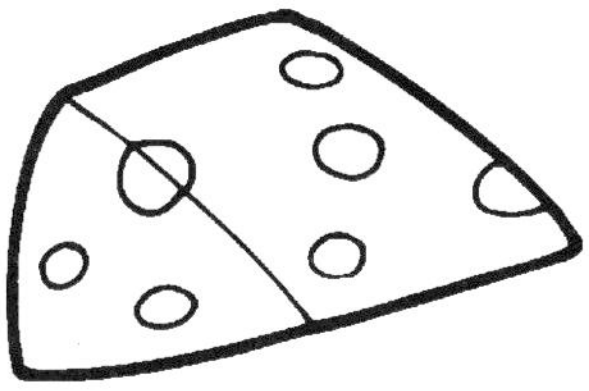

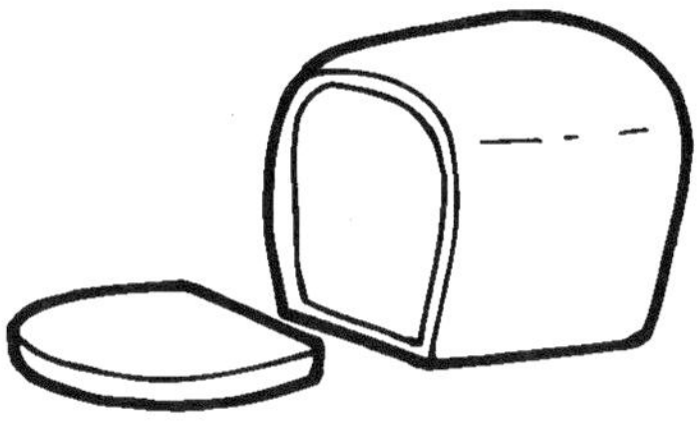

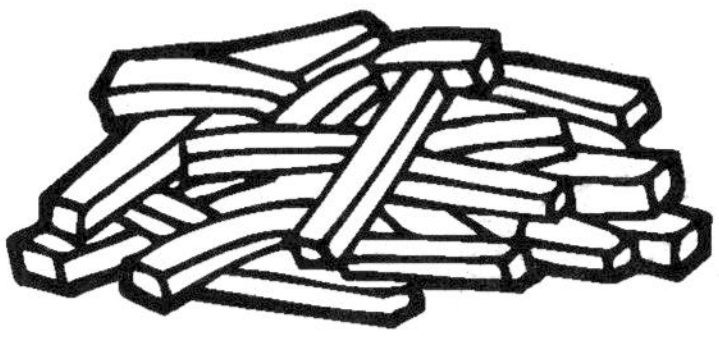

ch _ _ _ _   b _ _ _ _   ch _ _ _

Finish the sentences.

The food I like best is ______________________

because ______________________

____.

The food I don't like is ______________________

because ______________________

____.

Word Skills Copymaster 8

name ______________________ date ______________________

■ Sound the letters.
Trace and copy the letter pattern.

ill ill _______ _______ _______ _______

■ Write the word.
Colour the picture.

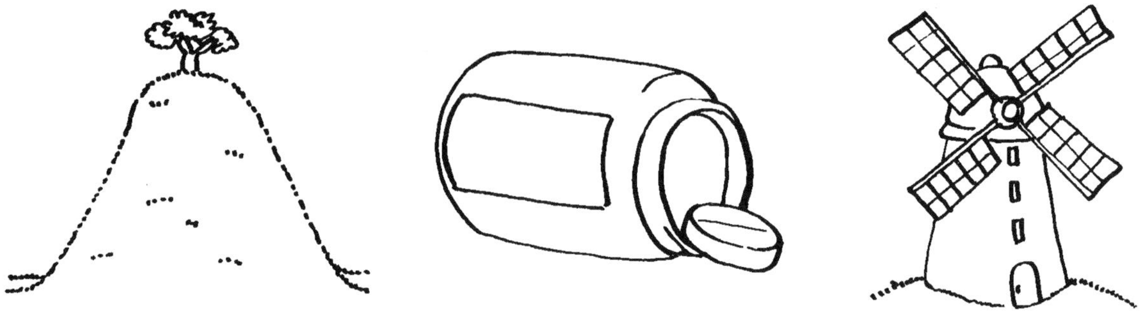

h__ __ __ p__ __ __ m__ __ __

■ For each word, write a rhyming word.
The pictures will help you.

will grill still

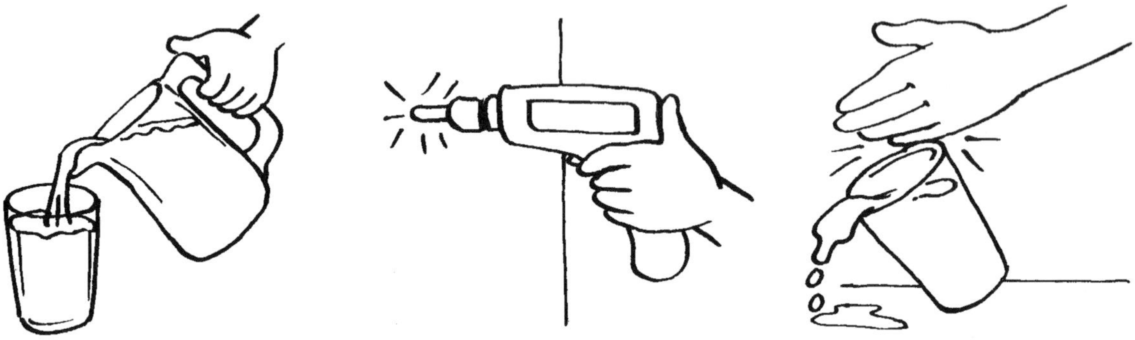

f__ __ __ d__ __ __ __ s__ __ __ __

Writing Copymaster 8

name ______________________ date ____________________

What would you like as a birthday surprise?

Draw it here.

Finish the sentence.

For my birthday surprise I would

like ________________________________

because ________________________________

____

____

name ______________________ date ______________________

Do the word sums.

Read the words you have made.

th + e = ______________________

th + en = ______________________

th + is = ______________________

th + at = ______________________

unit 8

th + em = ______________________

Make these words.

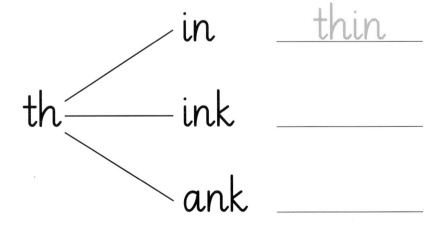

th — in thin

th — ink ______________________

th — ank ______________________

name ______________________ date ______________________

■ Who will you send the birthday card to?

What will you write inside?

Happy Birthday

■ Who will you invite to your party?

Fill in the party invitation.

____

is having a party!

The day ______________________

The date ______________________

The time ______________________

The place ______________________

name ______________________ date ______________________

■ Sound the letters.
Trace and copy the letter pattern.

ing ing ________ ________ ________ ________

■ Finish the words.
Colour the pictures.

r___ ___ ___ k___ ___ ___ s___ ___ ___

■ For each word, write a rhyming word.
The pictures will help you.

sing ring wing

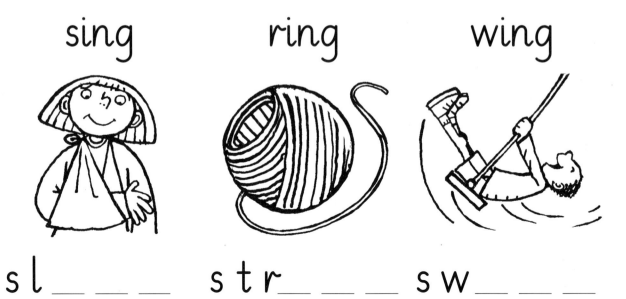

sl___ ___ ___ str___ ___ ___ sw___ ___ ___

unit 9

Nelson English

Writing Copymaster 9

Blue: Fiction

name ______________________ date ______________________

■ The children are flying the kite. Draw what happens next.

■ Write about what happens to the kite.

____

____

____

____

unit 9

name ______________________ date ______________________

What are the children doing?

Add ing to each word.

fly___ ___ ___

throw___ ___ ___

catch___ ___ ___

kick___ ___ ___

play___ ___ ___

walk___ ___ ___

Writing Copymaster 9

name ______________________ date ______________________

What do you like doing in the playground?

I like ____.

I like ____.

I like ____.

I like ____.

I like ____.

I like ____.

Write what the children are doing.

______________________ ______________________

______________________ ______________________

Word Skills Copymaster 10

Blue: Fiction

name ______________________ date ______________________

■ Sound the letters.

Trace and copy the letter pattern.

and and ______ ______ ______ ______

■ Write the word.

Colour the picture.

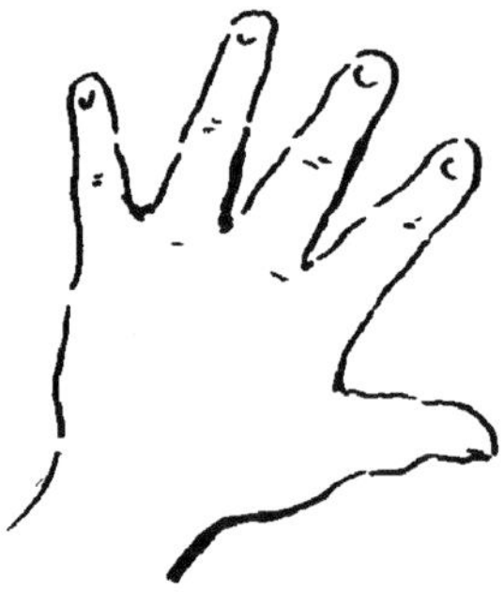

h___ ___ ___ s___ ___ ___ b___ ___ ___

■ Copy the sentence.

Let's stand and listen to the band.

____

____

Writing Copymaster 10

Blue: Fiction

name ______________________ date ______________________

■ Finish the sentences.

Sand gets in your ____________.

Sand gets in your ____________.

■ Write a caption for each picture.

____

____

____

____

unit 10

Word Skills Copymaster 10

Blue: Non-fiction

name ______________________ date ______________________

■ Sound the letters.

Trace and copy the letter pattern.

end end ______ ______ ______ ______

■ Write an *end* word to go with each picture.

s p _ _ _

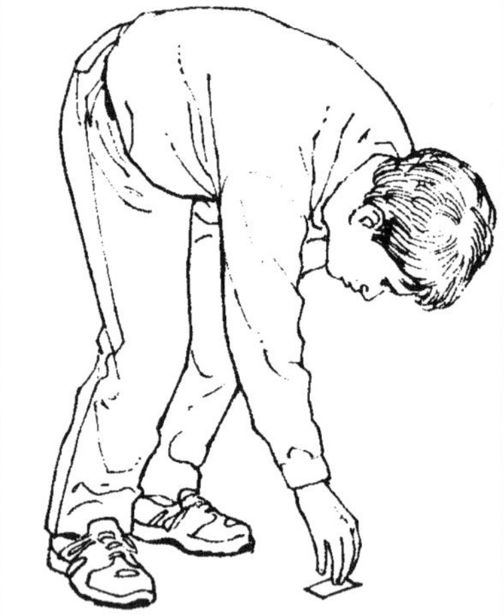

b _ _ _

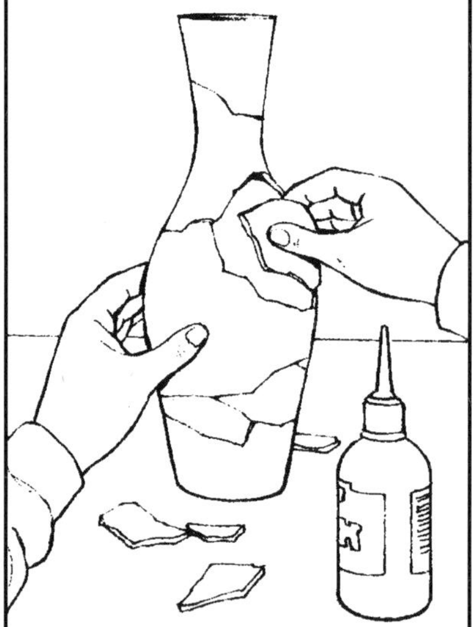

m _ _ _

■ Copy the sentence.

Sam is sending a postcard.

____

Nelson English

Writing Copymaster 10

Blue: Non-fiction

name ______________________ date ______________________

■ Where would you like to spend a holiday?

Draw a picture on this postcard.

■ Who will you send your postcard to?

Write a message. | Write the name and address.

Dear ______________

unit 10

name ____________________ date ____________________

Fill in the missing words.

Choose words from the box.

on	up	in	down

Roger and his mum came ________.

Mum put Roger ________ the rug.

The baby threw Mrs Pepperpot

________ in the air.

unit 11

Mrs Pepperpot fell ________.

Writing Copymaster 11

name ______________________ date ______________________

Write what is happening in each picture.

In the last box, draw what happens next.

Word Skills Copymaster 11

name ______________________ date ______________________

The **b**aby likes **b**iscuits.
Sam likes **s**wimming.
Daisy likes **d**ogs.

Write your name.

____

Draw four things you like that start with the same sound as your name.
Write the word under each picture.

name ______________________ date ______________________

Bouncing **B**abies love **B**essie's **B**aby **B**iscuits!

Can you think of another 'b' word to describe babies?

b ______________ babies

Can you think of another 'b' word to describe biscuits?

b ______________ biscuits

Colour the pictures.

Think of two other words beginning with the same letter to describe each item.

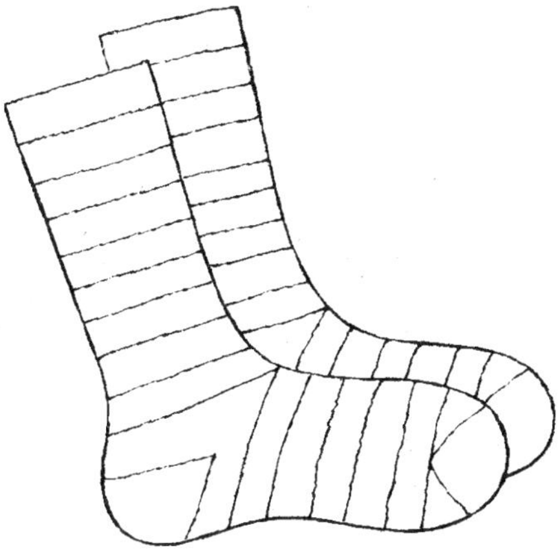

s ______________,

s ______________

socks

b ______________,

b ______________

bike

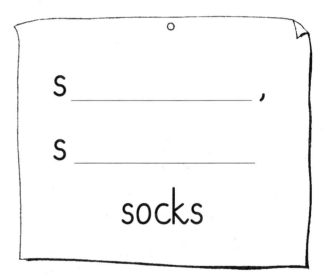

name ______________________ date ______________________

Fill in the missing words.
Choose words from the box.

in	down	on	up

We were ________

the hall.

We sat ________

the mats.

Tim climbed ________

the rope.

"Get ________!"

said the teacher.

Writing Copymaster 12

name ______________________ date ______________________

Write about what is happening in the picture.

Nelson English

Word Skills Copymaster 12

Blue: Non-fiction

name ______________________ date ______________________

What are they doing?

Add ing to each word.

read ___ ___ ___

colour ___ ___ ___

draw ___ ___ ___

cook ___ ___ ___

count ___ ___ ___

build ___ ___ ___

stick ___ ___ ___

weigh ___ ___ ___

paint ___ ___ ___

Writing Copymaster 12

name ______________________ date ______________________

■ Put the pictures in the correct order.

■ Finish the sentence.

The pictures show ______________________

____

____.

Letter Skills Copymaster 1

name ______________________ date ______________________

Trace over the letters.

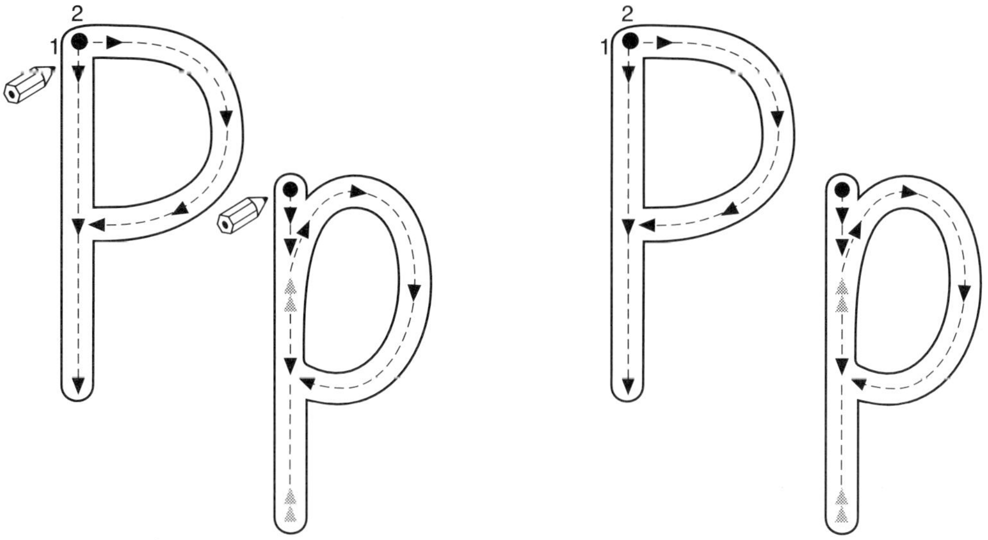

Trace and then copy the letters.

P

p

Write the missing letter in each word.

_an

_en

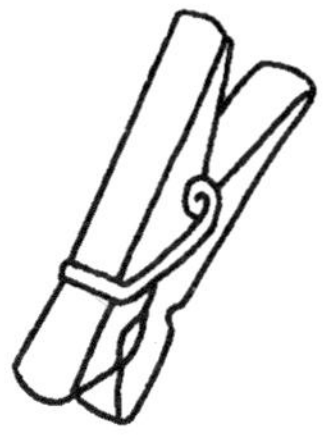

_eg

_in

Letter Skills Copymaster 2

name ______________________ date ______________________

■ Trace over the letters.

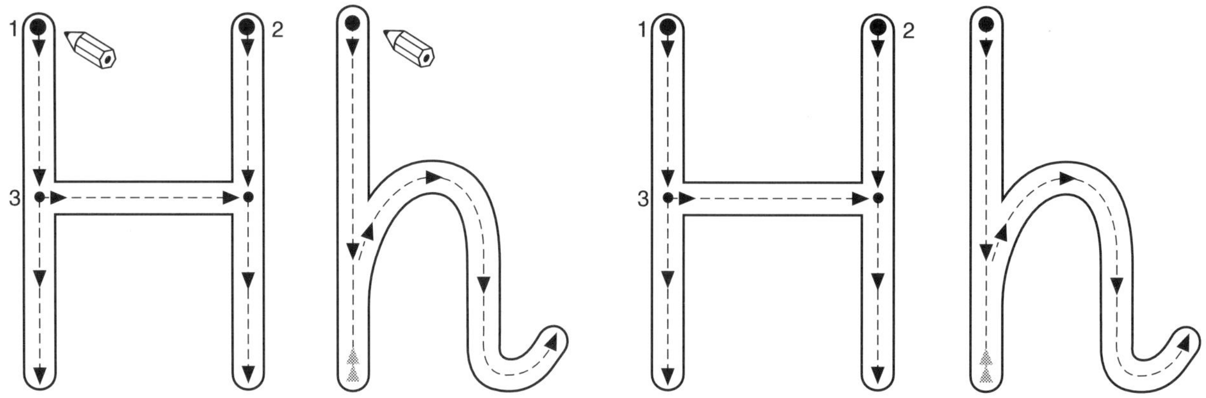

■ Trace and then copy the letters.

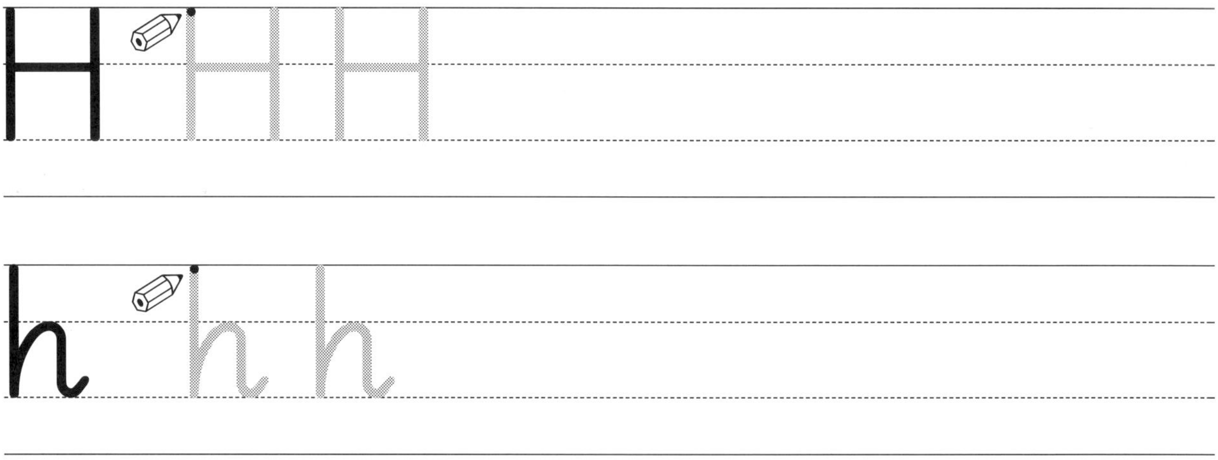

■ Write the missing letter in each word.

__en

__at

__it

__op

Nelson English

Letter Skills Copymaster 3

Blue Level

name ____________________ date ____________________

3

Trace over the letters.

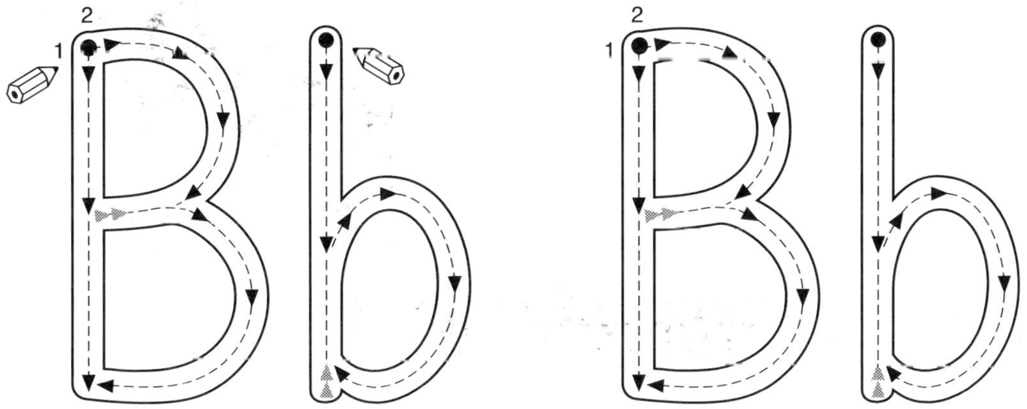

Trace and then copy the letters.

B B B

b b b

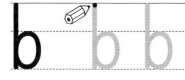

Write the missing letter in each word.

__ed

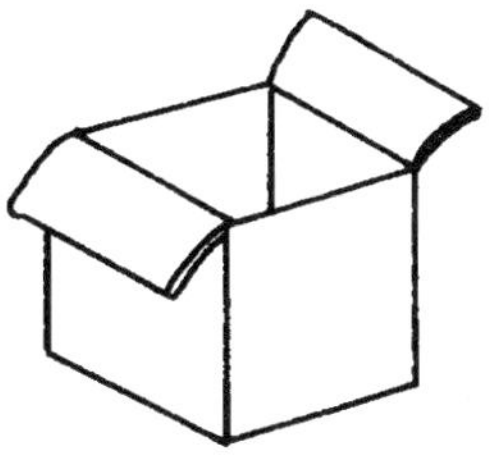

__ox

__at

__ug

name ______________________ date ______________________

4

Trace over the letters.

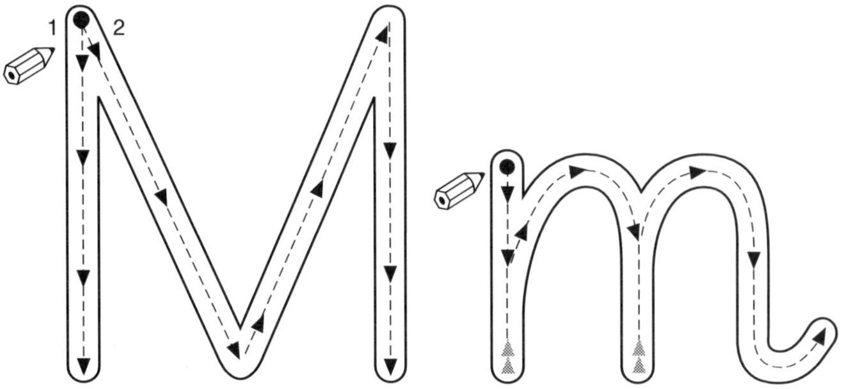

Trace and then copy the letters.

M M M

m m m

Write the missing letter in each word.

_an

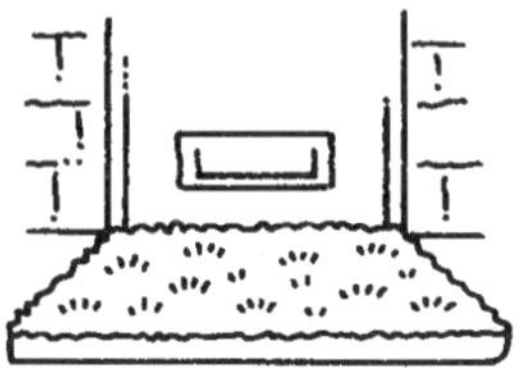

_at

_ug

_op

Letter Skills Copymaster 5

Blue Level

name ______________________ date ______________________

5

■ Trace over the letters.

C c C c

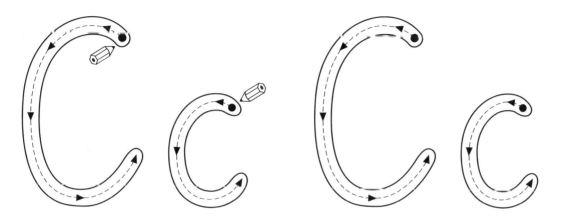

■ Trace and then copy the letters.

C C C

c c c

■ Write the missing letter in each word.

_at

_up

_ar

_ot

Letter Skills Copymaster 6

name ______________________ date ______________________

6

■ Trace over the letters.

■ Trace and then copy the letters.

S S S

s s s

■ Write the missing letter in each word.

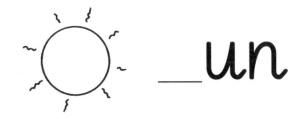

6 _ix

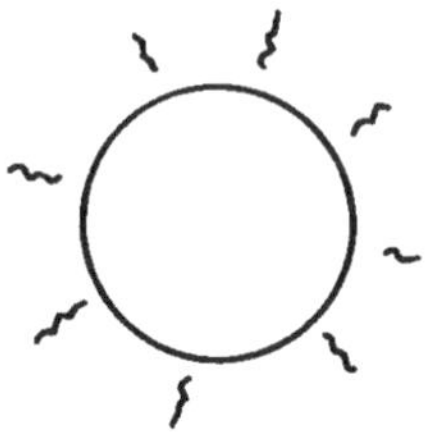

_un

_aw

_it

Nelson English

Letter Skills Copymaster 7

Blue Level

name ______________________ date ______________________

Trace over the letters.

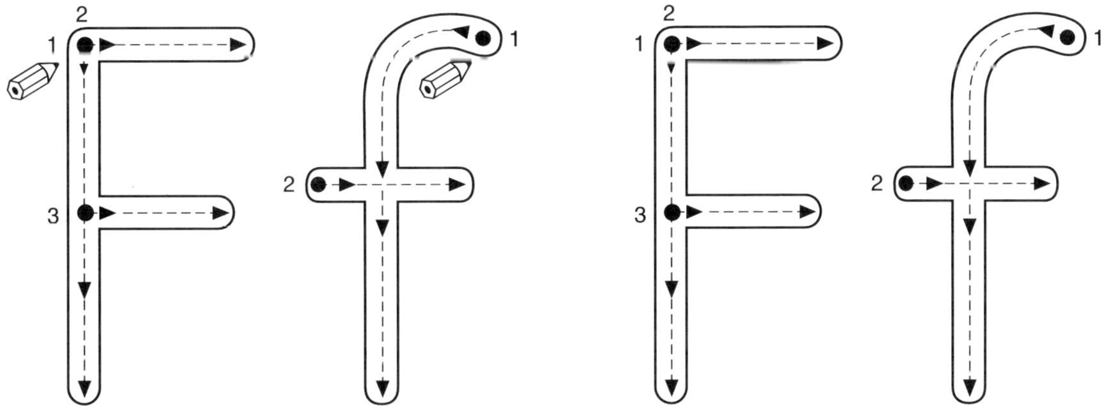

7

Trace and then copy the letters.

Write the missing letter in each word.

__ox

__an

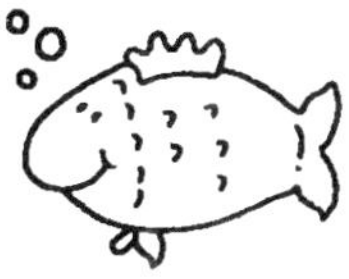

__ish

__rog

Nelson English

Letter Skills Copymaster 8

Blue Level

name ______________________ date ______________________

8

■ Trace over the letters.

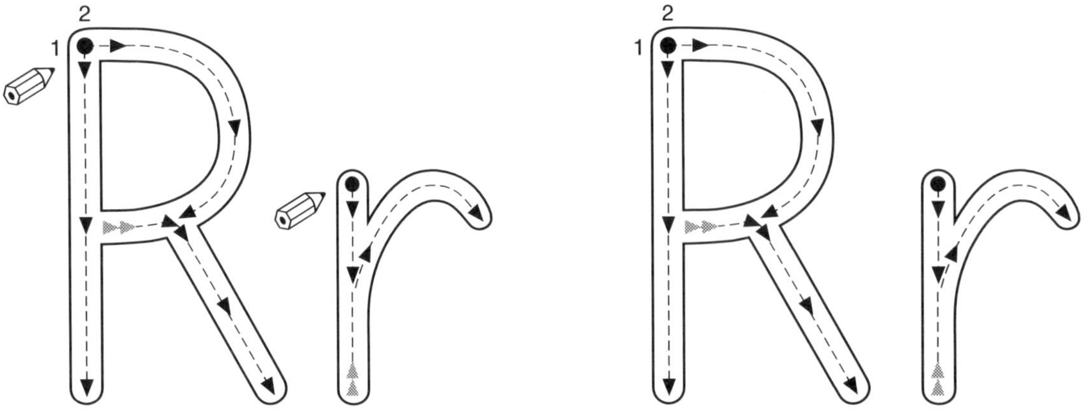

■ Trace and then copy the letters.

R R R

r r r

■ Write the missing letter in each word.

__at

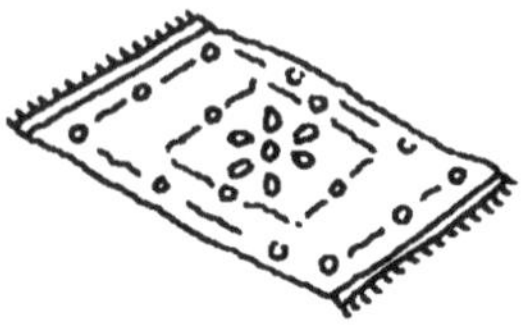

__ug

__un

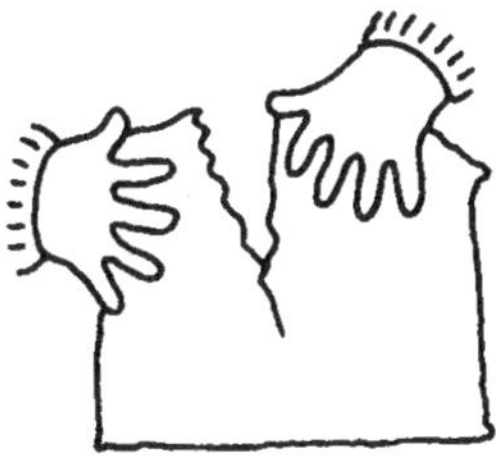

__ip

Nelson English

Letter Skills Copymaster 9

Blue Level

name ______________________ date ______________________

Trace over the letters.

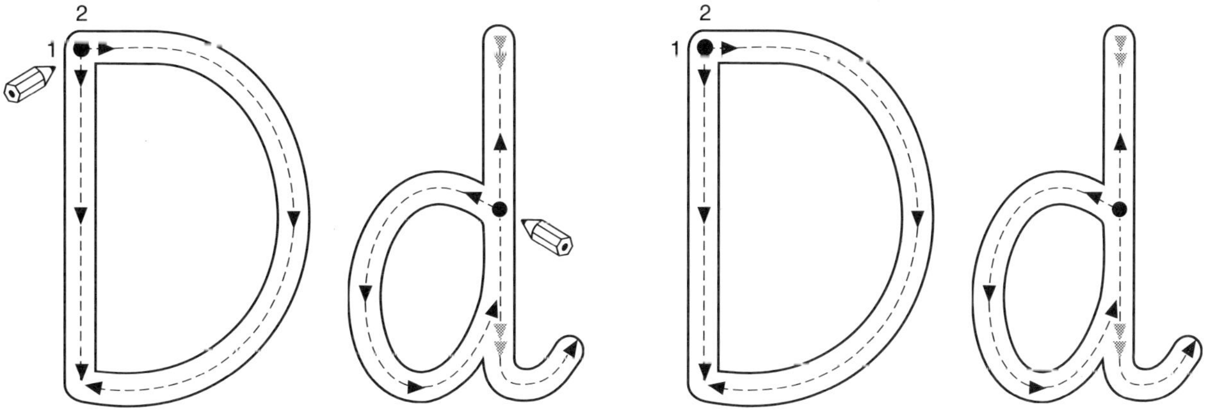

9

Trace and then copy the letters.

D D D

d d d

Write the missing letter in each word.

_og

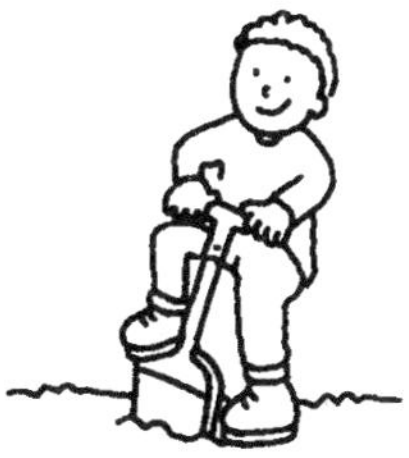

_ig

_art

_uck

Nelson English

Letter Skills Copymaster 10

Blue Level

name ______________________ date ______________________

Trace over the letters.

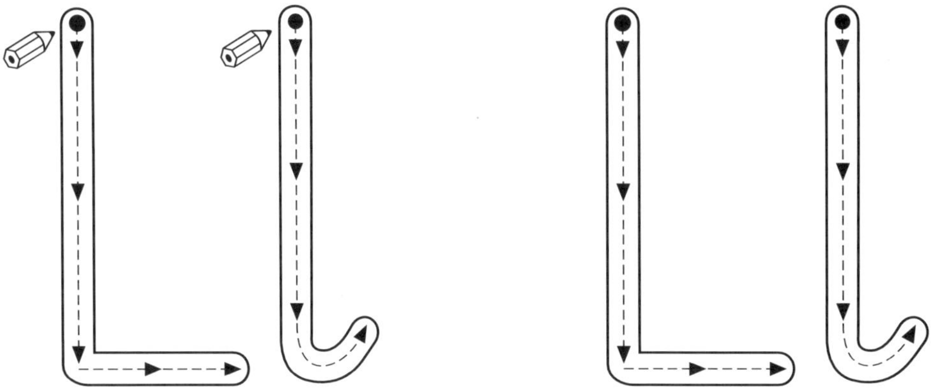

10

Trace and then copy the letters.

Write the missing letter in each word.

__og

__eg

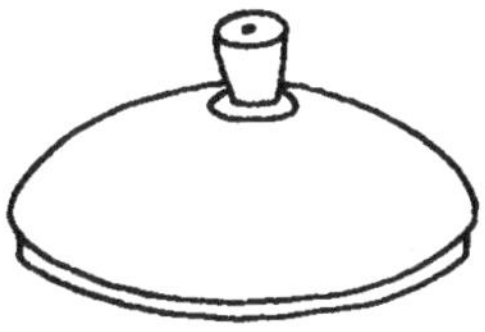

__id

__ion

Letter Skills Copymaster 11

Blue Level

name ______________________ date ______________________

Trace over the letters.

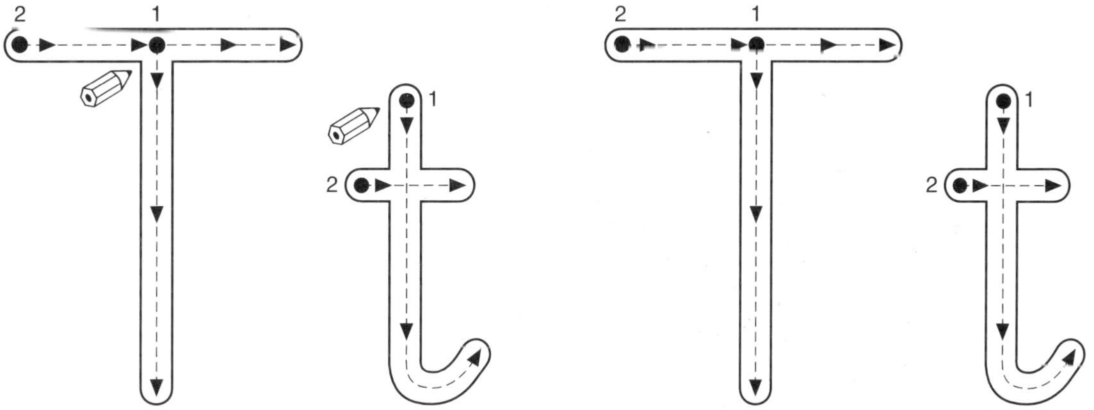

Trace and then copy the letters.

Write the missing letter in each word.

_ap

10 _en

_in

_ent

Nelson English

Letter Skills Copymaster 12

Blue Level

name ______________________ date ______________________

■ Trace over the letters.

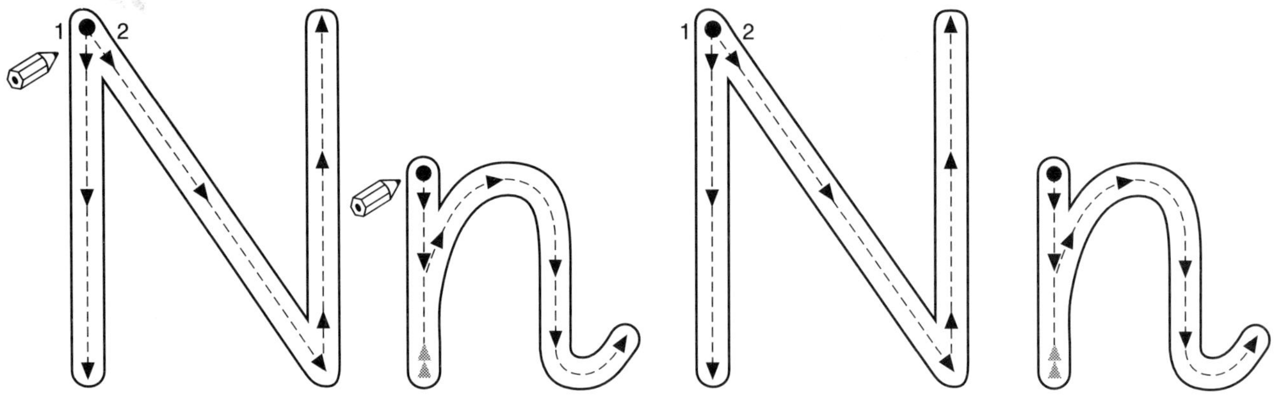

■ Trace and then copy the letters.

12

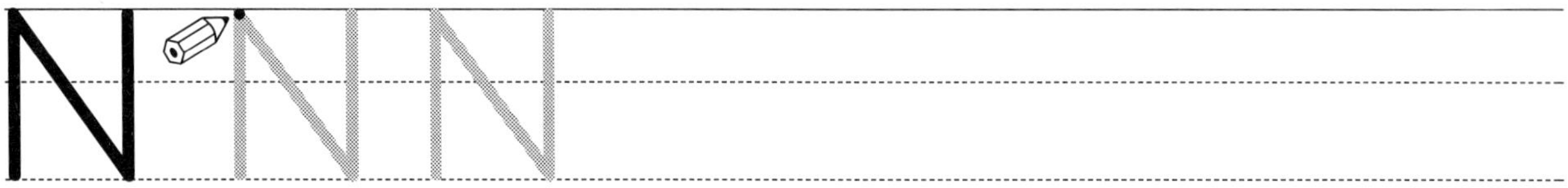

■ Write the missing letter in each word.

__et

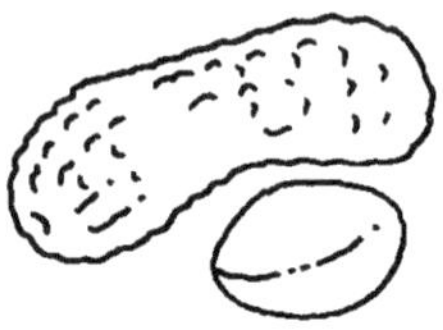

__ut

__ap

__ip

name ______________________ date ______________________

■ Trace over the letters.

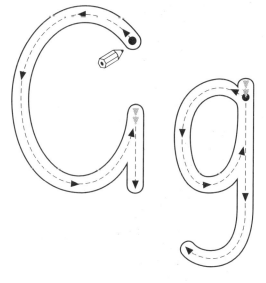

G g G g

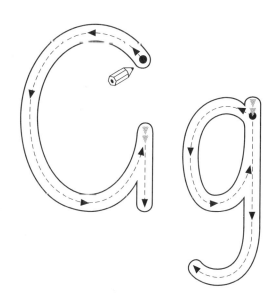

■ Trace and then copy the letters.

G G G

g g g

13

■ Write the missing letter in each word.

_ap

_ift

_irl

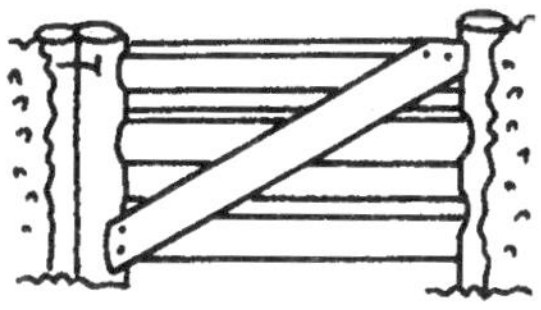

_ate

Nelson English

Letter Skills Copymaster 14

Blue Level

name ______________________ date ______________________

■ Trace over the letters.

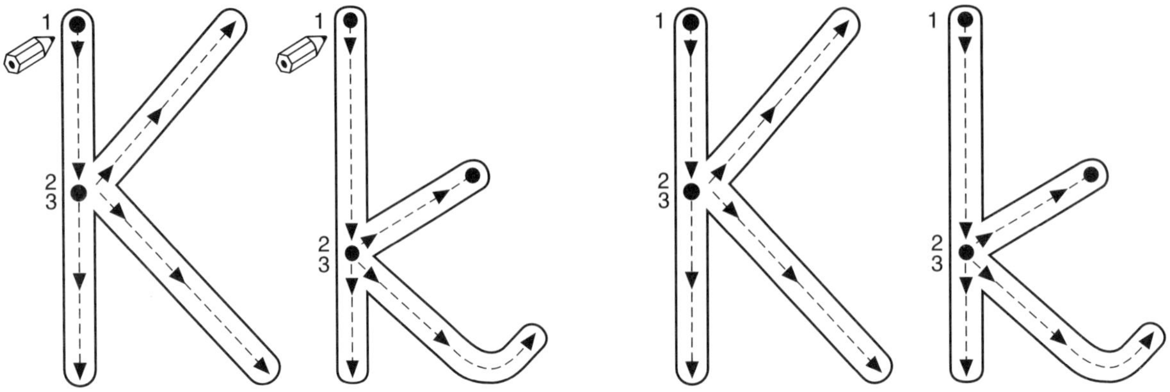

■ Trace and then copy the letters.

K K K

k k k

■ Write the missing letter in each word.

_ey

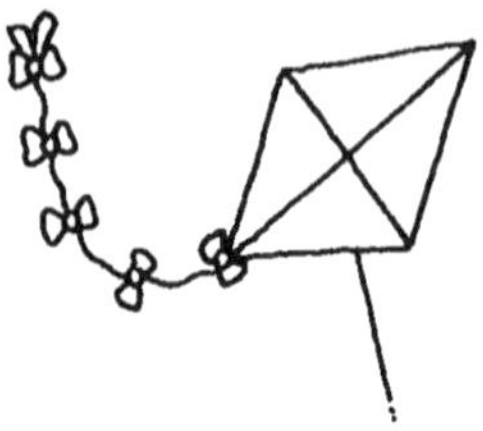

_ite

_iss

_ick

Nelson English

Letter Skills Copymaster 15

Blue Level

name ______________________ date ______________________

■ Trace over the letters.

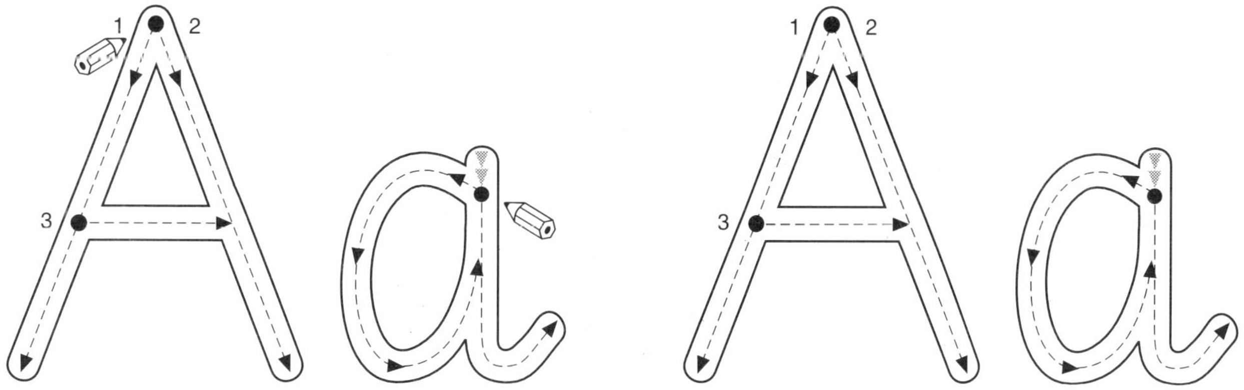

■ Trace and then copy the letters.

■ Write *a* next to each thing that begins with ‘a’.

Letter Skills Copymaster 16

Blue Level

name ______________________ date ______________________

■ Trace over the letters.

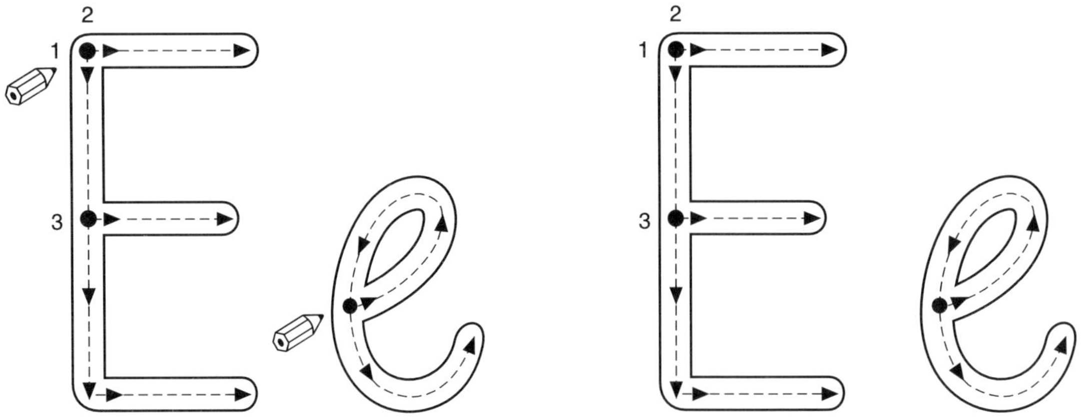

■ Trace and then copy the letters.

■ Write e next to each thing that begins with 'e'.

Letter Skills Copymaster 17

Blue Level

name ______________________ date ______________________

Trace over the letters.

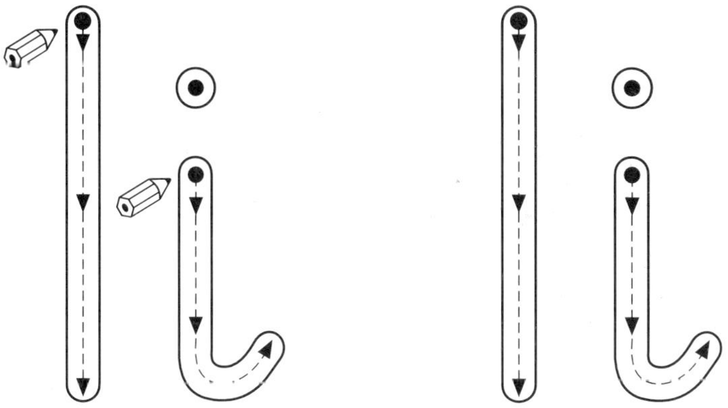

Trace and then copy the letters.

l

i

Write i next to each thing that begins with 'i'.

17

name ______________________ date ______________________

■ Trace over the letters.

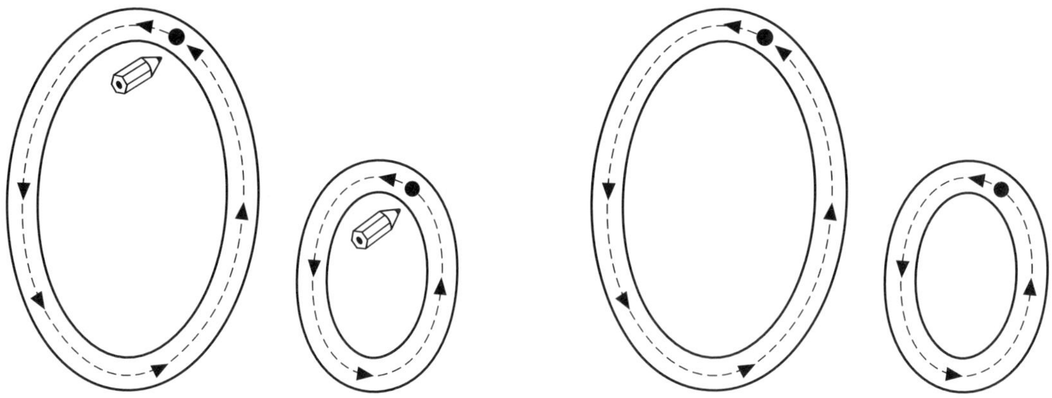

■ Trace and then copy the letters.

■ Write o next to each thing that begins with 'o'.

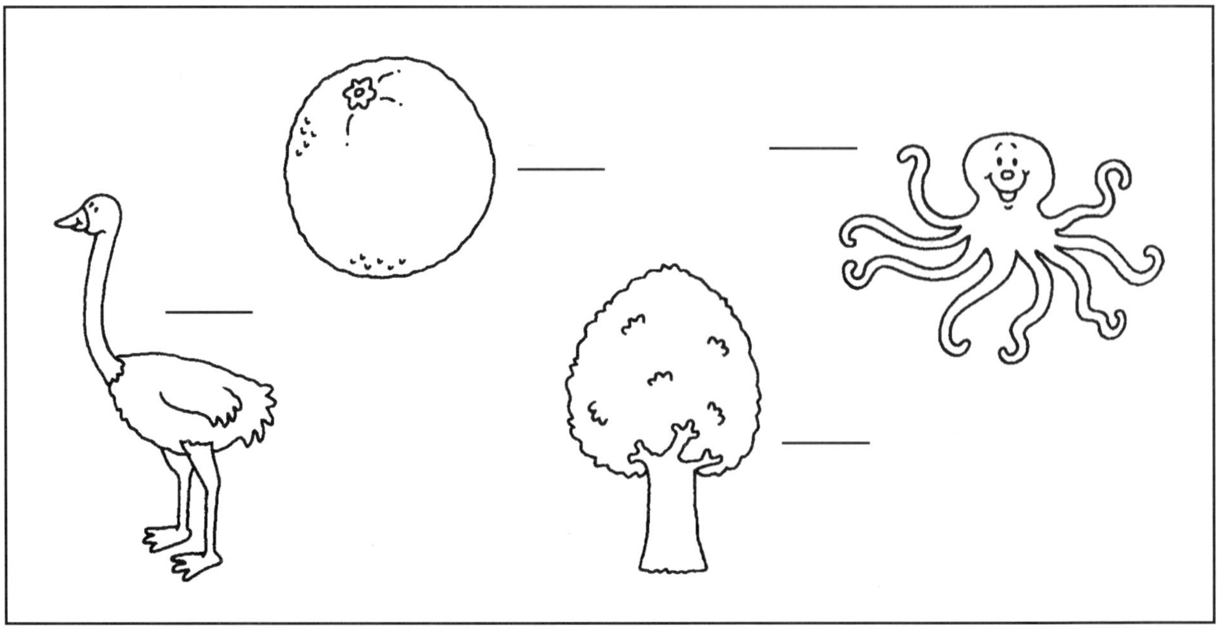

Nelson English

Letter Skills Copymaster 19

Blue Level

name ______________________ date ______________________

■ Trace over the letters.

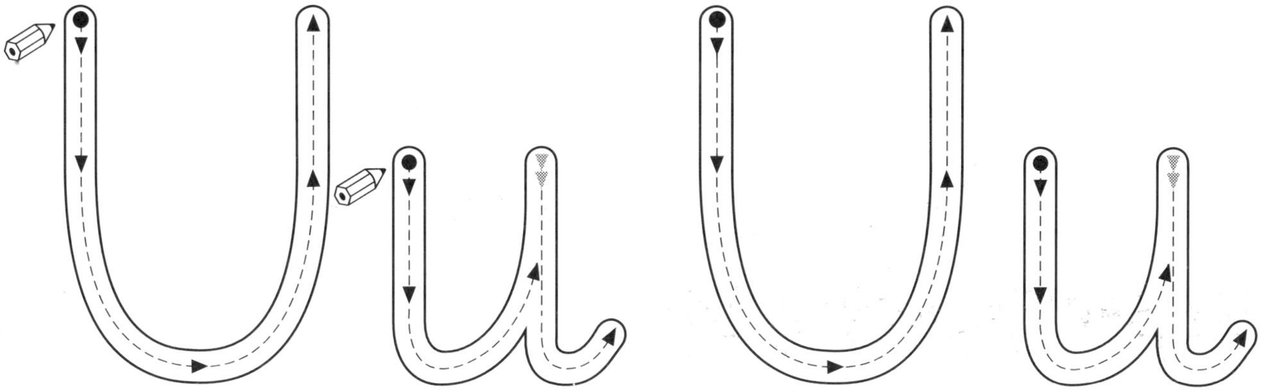

■ Trace and then copy the letters.

U U U

u u u

■ Write u next to each thing that begins with 'u'.

19

Nelson English

Letter Skills Copymaster 20

Blue Level

name ______________________ date ______________________

■ Trace over the letters.

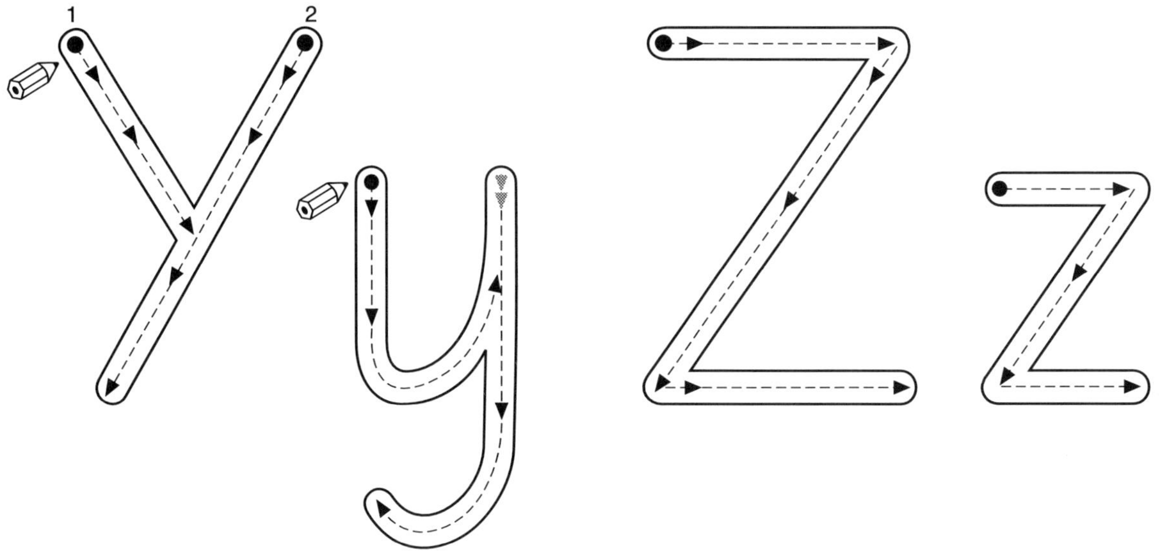

■ Trace and then copy the letters.

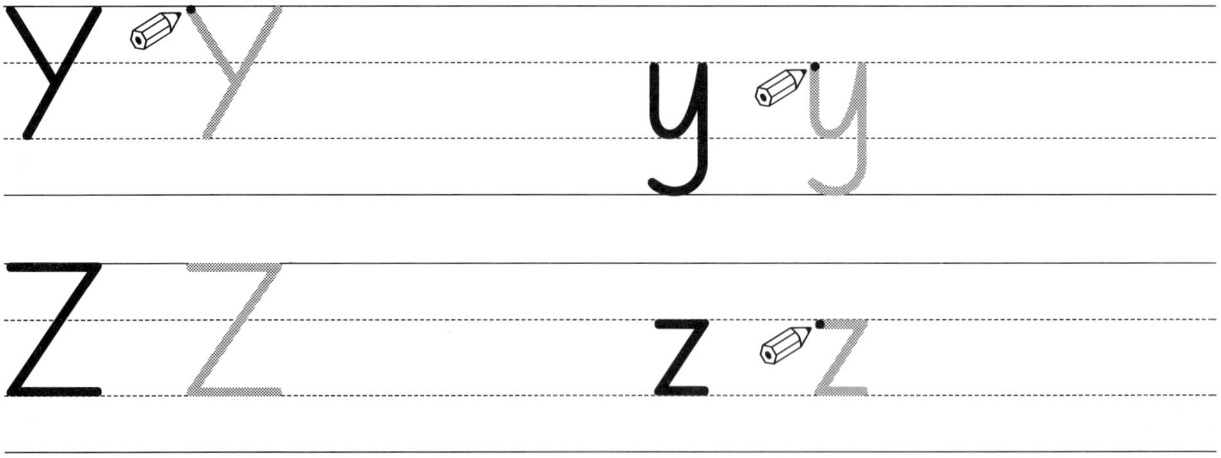

■ Write the missing letter in each word.

20

_ak

_o-yo

_ip

_ebra

name ______________________ date ______________________

Trace over the letters.

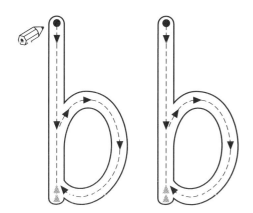

b b d d

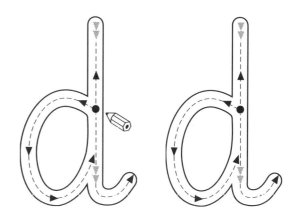

Trace and then copy the letters.

b b b

d d d

Colour in blue things beginning with '**b**'. Write b next to each. Colour in red things beginning with '**d**'. Write d next to each.

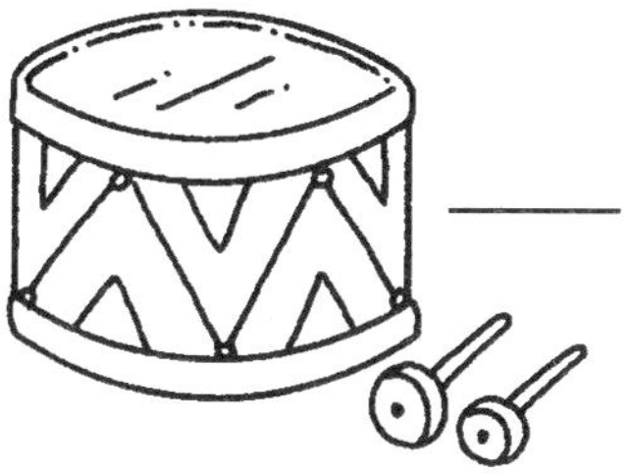

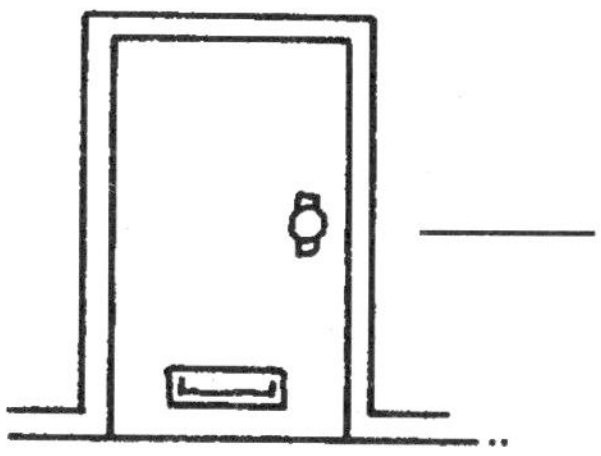

Nelson English

Letter Skills Copymaster 22

Blue Level

name ______________________ date ______________________

■ Trace over the letters.

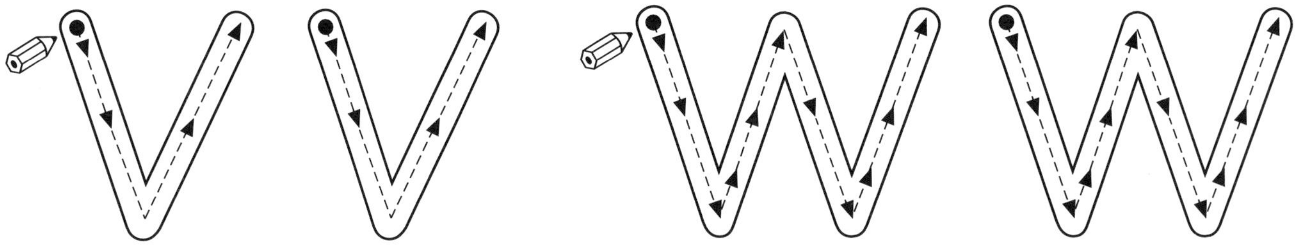

■ Trace and then copy the letters.

■ Colour in blue things beginning with '**v**'. Write v next to each.
Colour in red things beginning with '**w**'. Write w next to each.

 ____

 ____

 ____

 ____

 ____

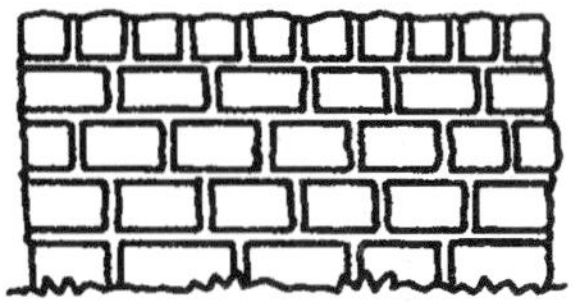 ____

Letter Skills Copymaster 23

Blue Level

name ______________________ date ______________________

Trace over the letters.

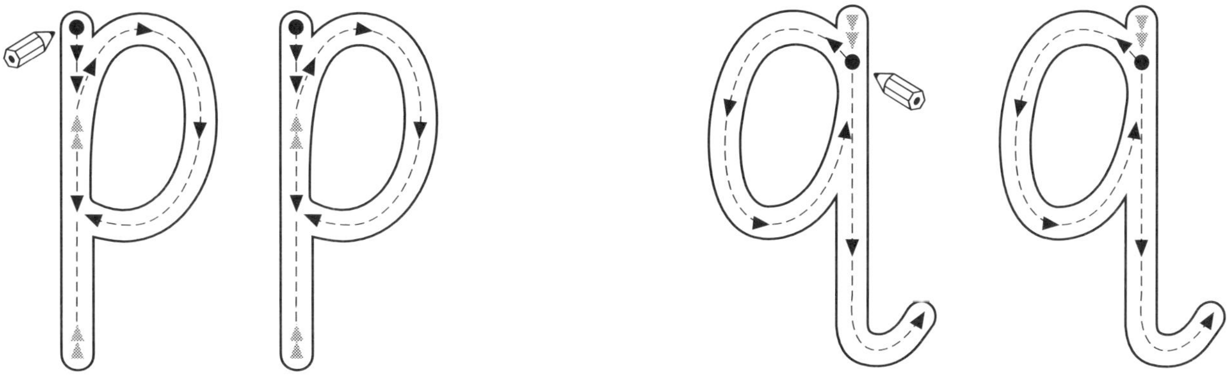

Trace and then copy the letters.

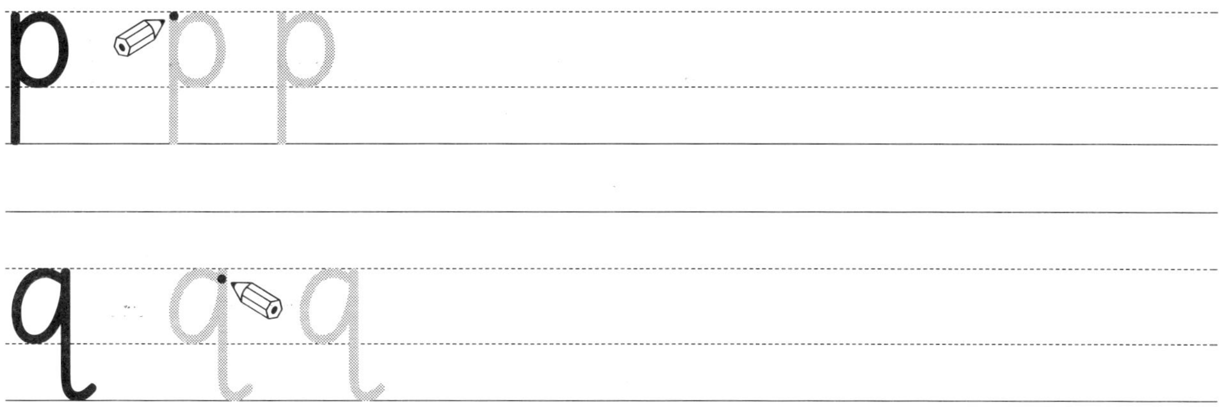

Colour in blue things beginning with '**p**'. Write p next to each. Colour in red things beginning with '**q**'. Write q next to each.

 ____

 ____

 ____

____ 

 ____

____ 

Nelson English

Letter Skills Copymaster 24

Blue Level

name ______________________ date ______________________

■ Trace over the letters.

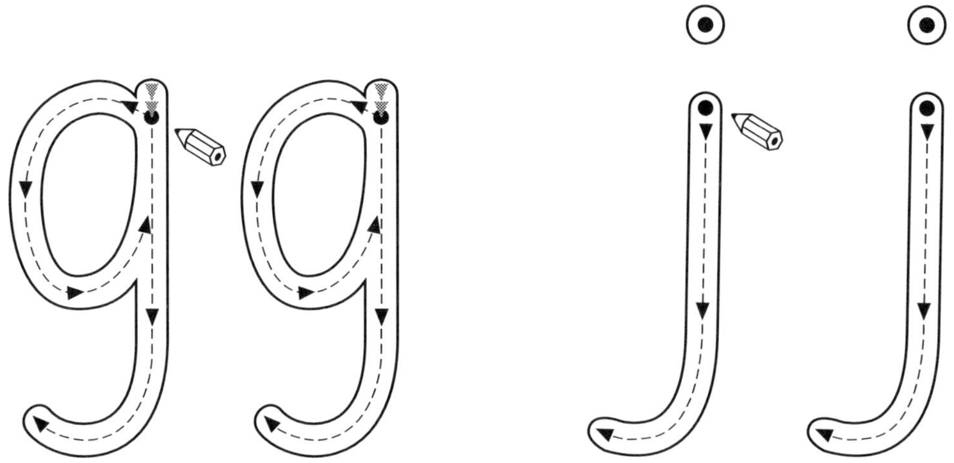

■ Trace and then copy the letters.

■ Colour in blue things beginning with '**g**'. Write g next to each.
Colour in red things beginning with '**j**'. Write j next to each.

 ____

____

 ____

 ____

 ____

 ____

Letter Skills Copymaster 25

Blue Level

name ______________________ date ______________________

■ Trace over the letters.

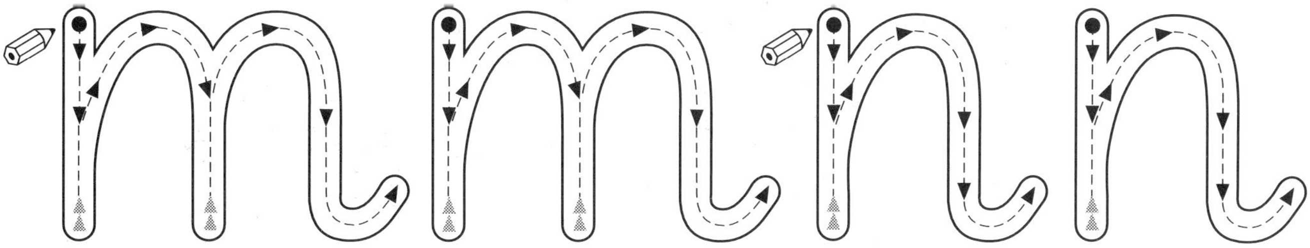

■ Trace and then copy the letters.

m m m

n n n

■ Colour in blue things beginning with '**m**'. Write m next to each.
Colour in red things beginning with '**n**'. Write n next to each.

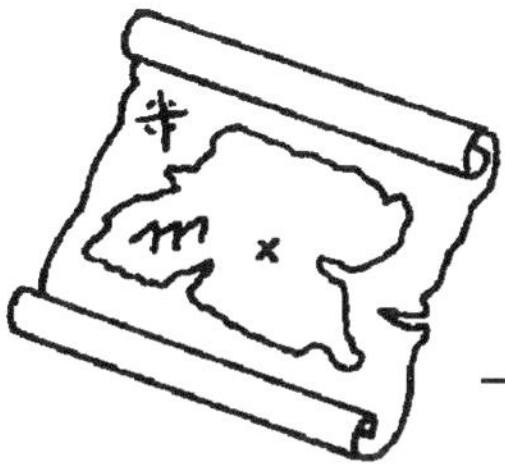

name ______________________ date ______________________

One Hot Day

I heard roaring,
One hot day.
Great, big teeth,
I ran away!

I heard hissing,
One hot day.
Long, red tongue,
I ran away!

I heard chattering,
One hot day.
Smiling face,
I stayed to play!

Nelson English

Poster Copymaster 1

Blue: Non-fiction

unit 1

name ______________________ date ______________________

name ______________________ date ______________________

Who's in?

'The door is shut fast
  And everyone's out!'
But people don't know
  What they're talking about!
Say the fly on the wall,
And the flame on the coals,
And the dog on his rug,
And the mice in their holes,
And the kitten curled up,
And the spiders that spin –
'What, everyone's out?
  Why, everyone's in!'

Nelson English

Poster Copymaster 2

Blue: Non-fiction

name ______________________ date ______________________

unit 2

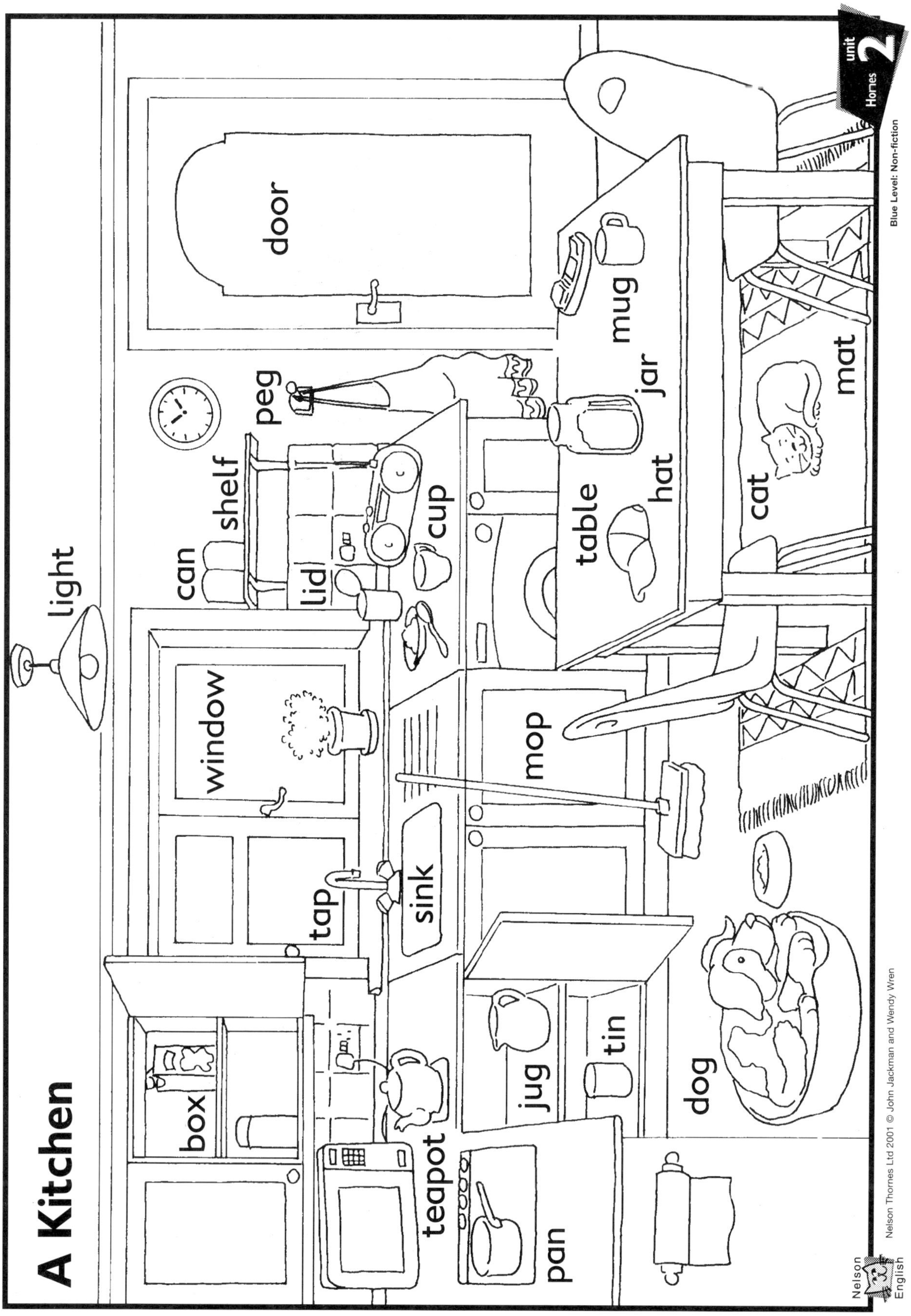

name ______________________ date ______________________

unit 3

A Little Bit of Colour

They ran down into the garden and Daniel said, “Tom, why don’t we paint the greenhouse? Not white like it is now, but all the colours of the rainbow!”

unit Colours 3

name ______________________ date ______________________

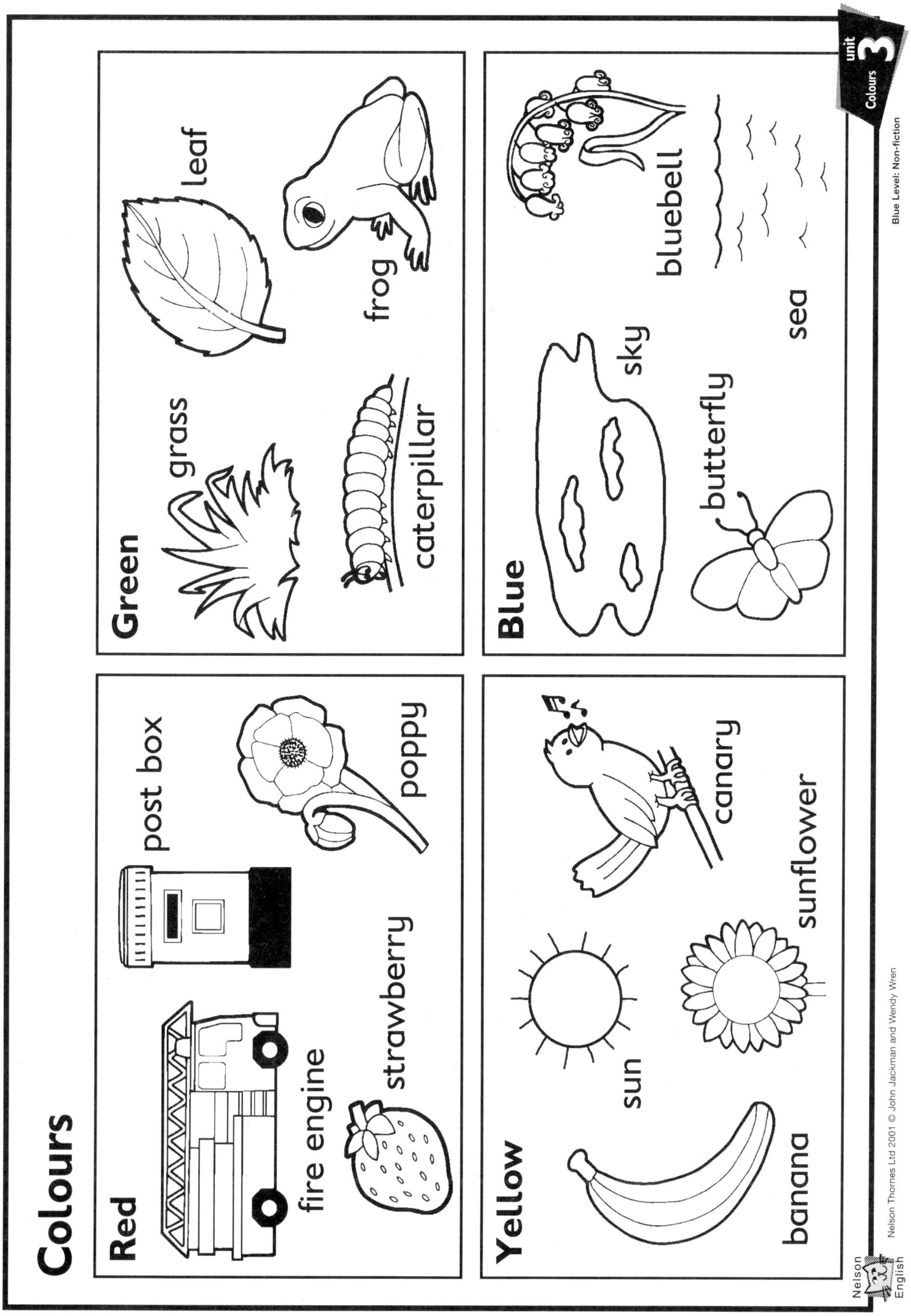
unit 3 Colours
Blue Level: Non-fiction
Colours
Red
fire engine
post box
strawberry
poppy
Green
grass
leaf
caterpillar
frog
Yellow
banana
sun
canary
sunflower
Blue
sky
bluebell
butterfly
sea
Nelson Thornes Ltd 2001 © John Jackman and Wendy Wren
Nelson English

name ______________________ date ______________________

I had a Little Cherry Stone

I had a little cherry stone
And put it in the ground,
And when next year I went to look,
A tiny shoot I found.

The shoot grew upwards day by day,
And soon became a tree.
I picked the rosy cherries then,
And ate them for my tea.

name ______________________ date ______________________

unit 4

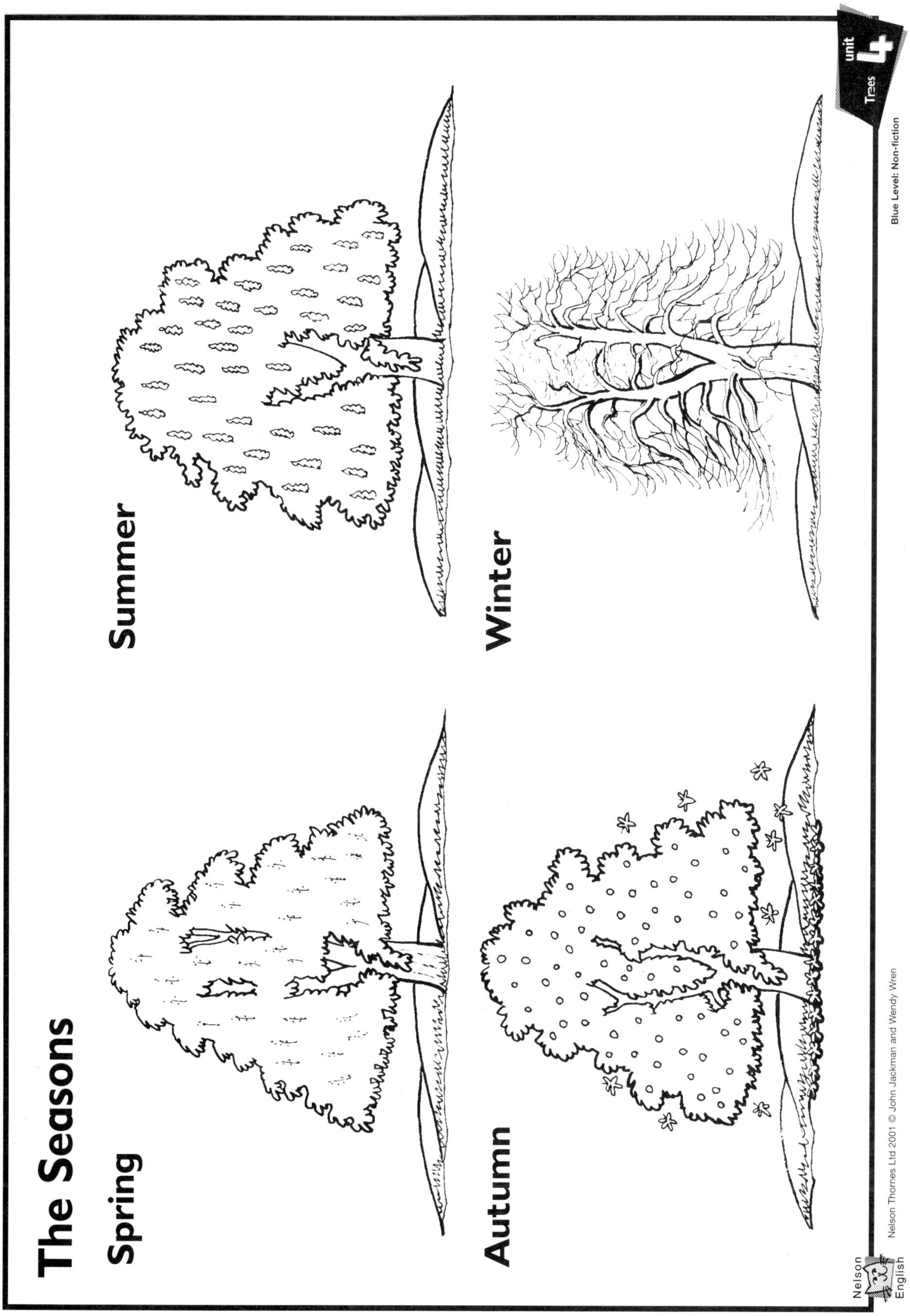
The Seasons
Spring
Summer
Autumn
Winter
unit 4
Trees
Blue Level: Non-fiction
Nelson Thornes Ltd 2001 © John Jackman and Wendy Wren
Nelson English

name ______________________ date ______________________

unit 5

New Shoes

My shoes are new and squeaky shoes,
They're very shiny, creaky shoes,
I wish I had my leaky shoes
That Mother threw away.

I liked my old, brown, leaky shoes
Much better than these creaky shoes,
These shiny, creaky, squeaky shoes
I've got to wear today.

unit Myself 5

Blue Level: Fiction

Nelson English

Poster Copymaster 5

Blue: Non-fiction

name ______________________ date ______________________

Myself

My name is ______________________.

I am ______ years old.

My hair is ______________________.

My eyes are ______________________.

I am ______ tall.

My favourite colour is ______________________.

My favourite food is ______________________.

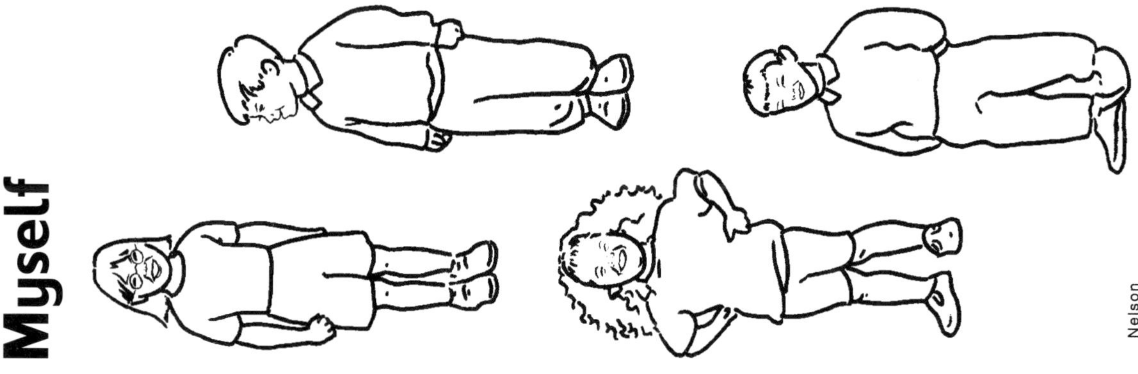

unit 5 Myself

Blue Level: Non-fiction

unit 5

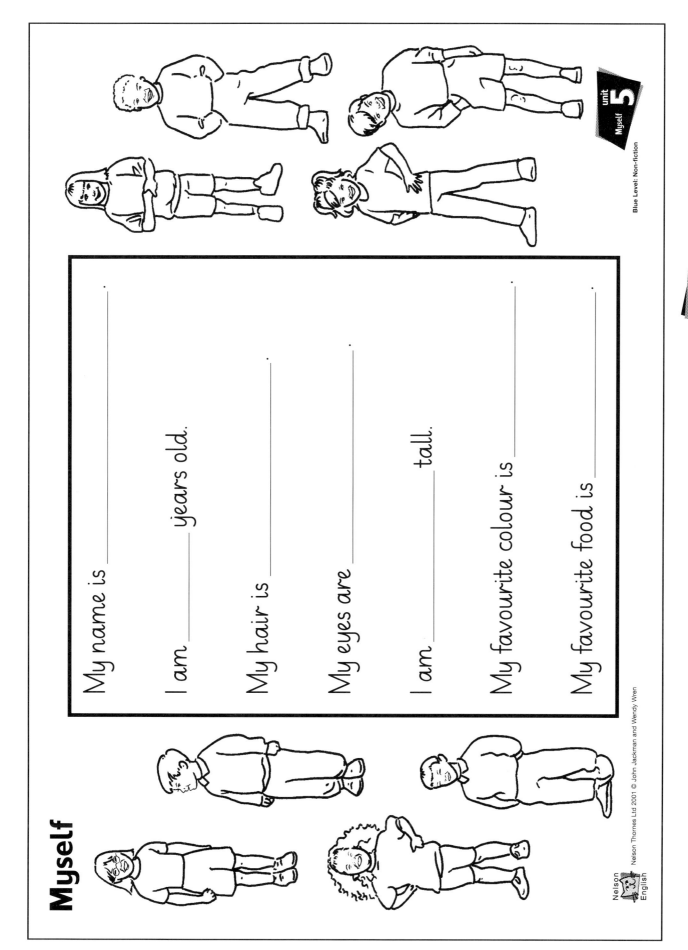

name ______________________ date ______________________

unit 6

Noah's Ark

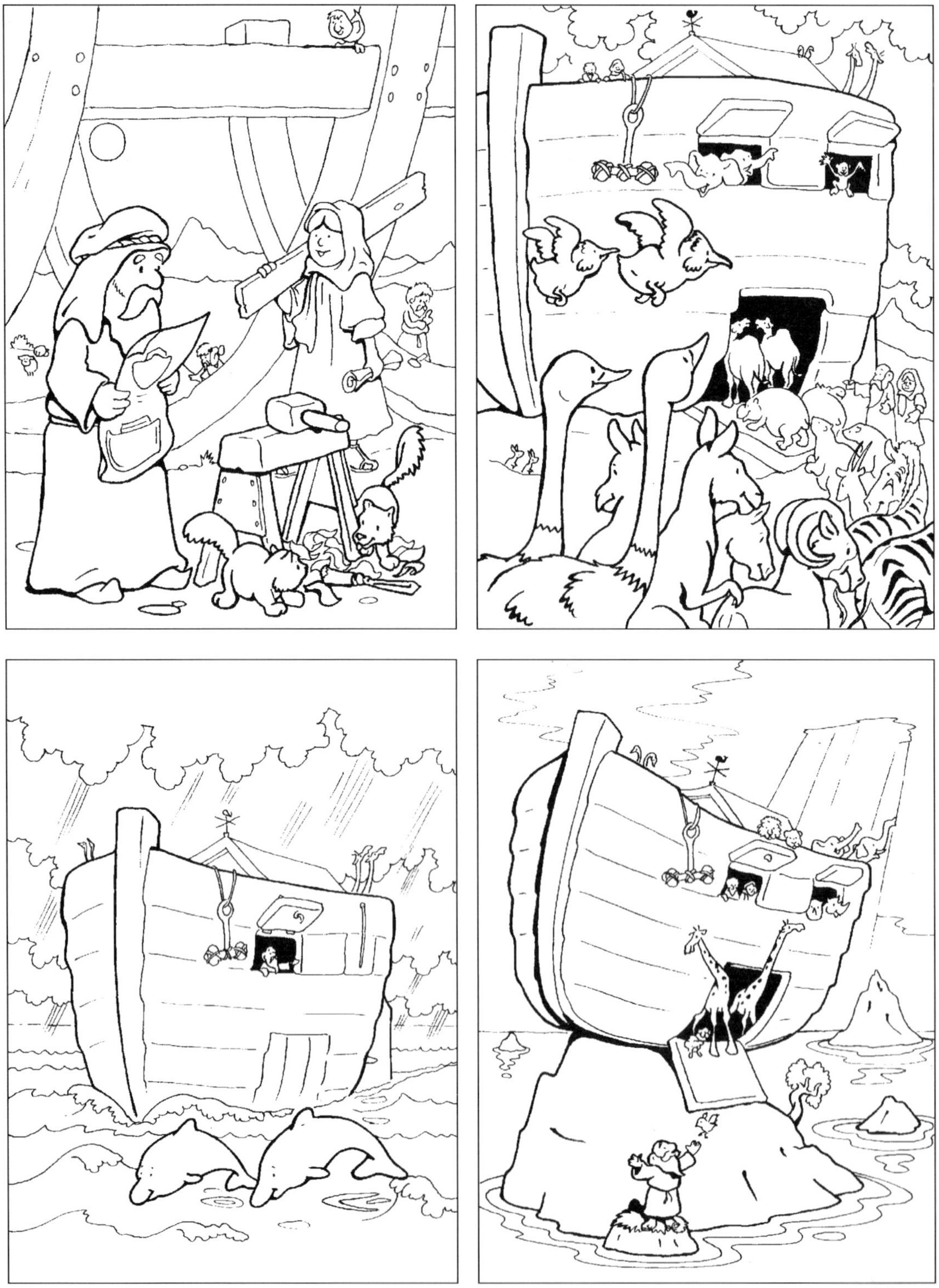

Nelson English

Blue Level: Fiction

unit Weather 6

name ______________________ date ______________________

The Weather

sun sunny
warm hot

cloud cloudy
dull grey

cold frosty
freezing icy
snowy

TODAY'S WEATHER

Day ______________________

Date ______________________

Month ______________________

Weather word ______________________

Weather picture

Weather sentence ______________________

____

wind windy
breezy gusty

fog foggy
mist misty

rain rainy
storm stormy
wet damp

unit 6 Weather

Blue Level: Non-fiction

Poster Copymaster 7

name ______________________ date ______________________

Ice Lolly

Red rocket
on a stick.
If it shines,
lick it quick.

Round the edges,
on the top,
round the bottom,
do not stop.
Suck the lolly,
lick your lips.
Lick the sides
as it drips
off the stick –
quick, quick,
lick, lick –
Red rocket
on a stick.

Nelson English

Poster Copymaster 7

Blue: Non-fiction

name ______________________ date ______________________

unit 7

name ______________________ date ______________________

Betsey's Birthday Surprise

The moment Betsey opened her eyes, she expected wonderful, sun-shiny, brilliant surprises.

Poster Copymaster 8

Blue: Non-fiction

name ______________________ date ______________________

Nelson English

Poster Copymaster 9

Blue: Fiction

name ______________________ date ______________________

The Kite

unit 9

name ______________________ date ______________________

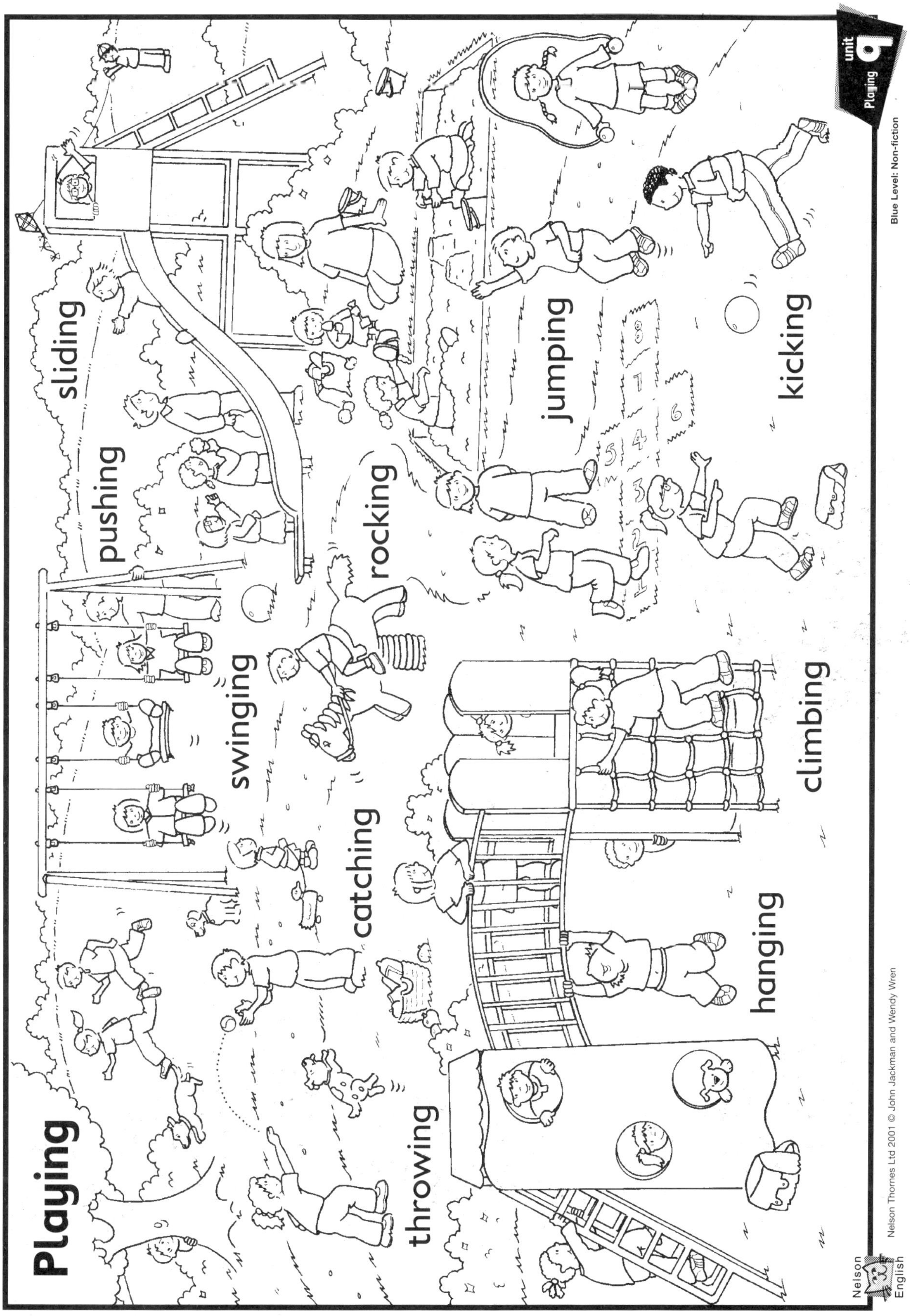

unit 9

name ____________________ date ____________________

Sand

Sand in your fingernails
Sand between your toes
Sand in your earholes
Sand up your nose!

Sand in your sandwiches
Sand on your bananas
Sand in your bed at night
Sand in your pyjamas!

Sand in your sandals
Sand in your hair
Sand in your knickers
Sand everywhere!

name ______________________ date ______________________

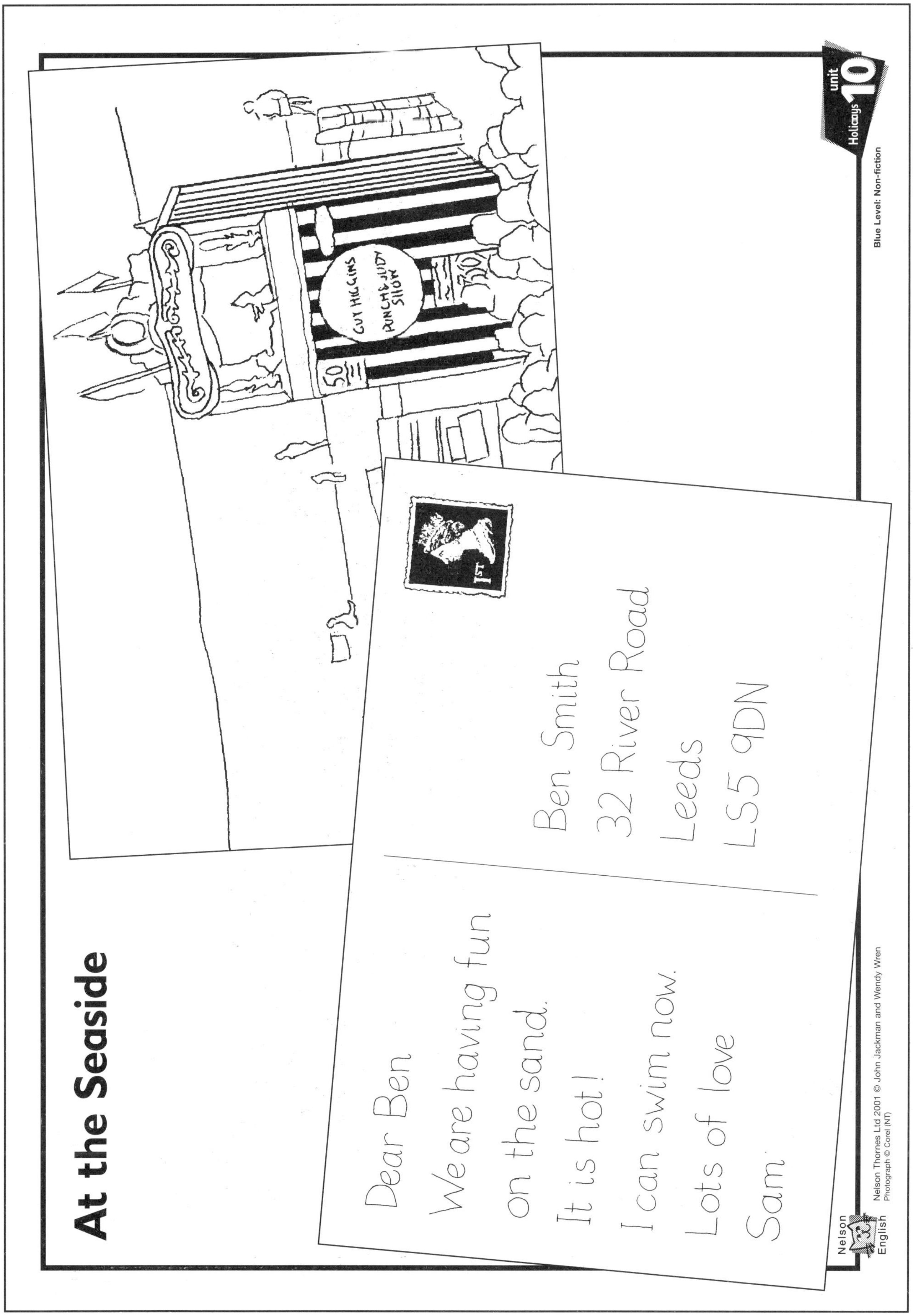
At the Seaside
unit 10 Holidays
Blue Level: Non-fiction
GUY HIGGINS PUNCH & JUDY SHOW
Dear Ben
We are having fun
on the sand.
It is hot!
I can swim now.
Lots of love
Sam
Ben Smith
32 River Road
Leeds
LS5 9DN
Nelson English
Nelson Thornes Ltd 2001 © John Jackman and Wendy Wren
Photograph © Corel (NT)

name ______________________ date ______________________

Mrs Pepperpot Looks After the Baby

Mrs Pepperpot has a strange problem. She is never sure when she is going to shrink to the size of a pepperpot!

name ______________________ date ______________________

Baby Food
Bouncing babies love
Bessie's Baby Biscuits!
unit 11
Babies
Blue Level: Non-fiction
Nelson English
Nelson Thornes Ltd 2001 © John Jackman and Wendy Wren
Photograph © Digital Vision (NT)

name ______________________ date ______________________

P.E.

Knees up,
legs stretch,
reach up tall!
Arms bend,
head down,
curl up in a ball!

Race now,
chase now,
left foot, hop!
Skip again,
scissor-jump,
and then
STOP!

Nelson English

Poster Copymaster 12

Blue: Non-fiction

name ______________________ date ______________________

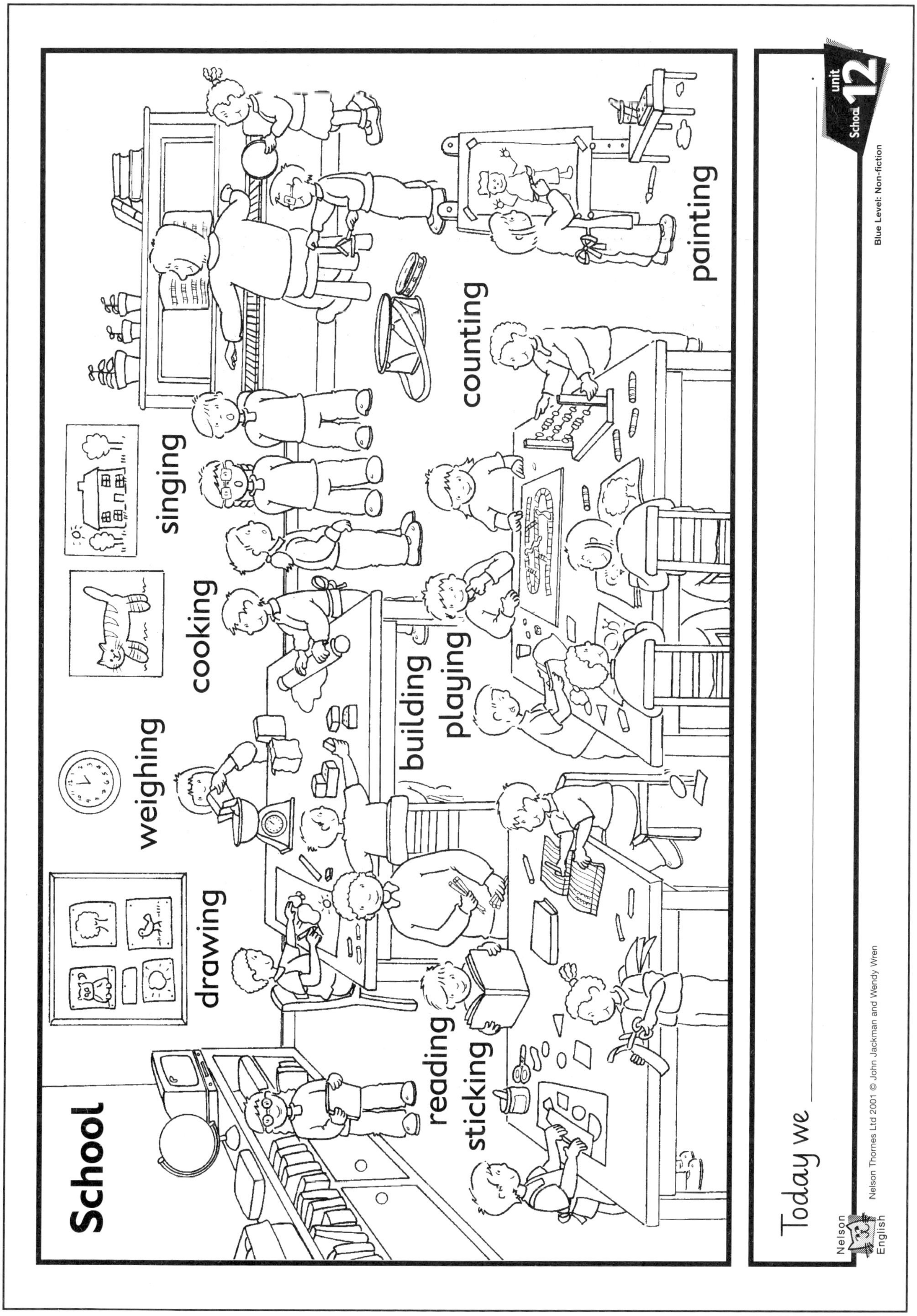

unit 12

Nelson English

Pupil Record Sheet
Blue Level (Reception)

Last name ______________________________

First name ______________________________

Key

☐ Activity undertaken

☒ Activity undertaken and understood

		Word skills	Writing	Letter Skills copymaster		Comments
Unit 1 Animals	Fiction			1		
	Non-fiction			2		
Unit 2 Homes	Fiction			3		
	Non-fiction			4		
Unit 3 Colours	Fiction			5		
	Non-fiction			6		
Unit 4 Trees	Fiction			7		
	Non-fiction			8		
Unit 5 Myself	Fiction			9		
	Non-fiction			10		
Unit 6 Weather	Fiction			11		
	Non-fiction			12		
Unit 7 Food	Fiction			13		
	Non-fiction			14		
Unit 8 Birthday	Fiction			15		
	Non-fiction			16		
Unit 9 Playing	Fiction			17		
	Non-fiction			18		
Unit 10 Holidays	Fiction			19		
	Non-fiction			20		
Unit 11 Babies	Fiction			21		
	Non-fiction			22		
Unit 12 School	Fiction			23		
	Non-fiction			24		
				25		